THE CHANGING PATTERNS OF THE MIDDLE EAST

The Changing Patterns of the Middle East

By

PIERRE RONDOT

FREDERICK A. PRAEGER
PUBLISHER
NEW YORK

Published in Great Britain by
Chatto and Windus Ltd
40–42 William IV Street
London W.C.2

*

Translated by Mary Dilke
from
Destin du Proche-Orient
Editions du Centurion
Paris, 1959

Published in the United States of America in 1961
by
Frederick A. Praeger, Inc., Publisher
15 West 47th Street, New York 36, N.Y.

Library of Congress Catalog Card Number: 61–10517

Printed in Great Britain by
Hazell Watson & Viney Ltd, Aylesbury and Slough

CONTENTS

FOREWORD

AMONG THE MANY persons who have contributed directly or indirectly to the writing of this book, and to whom I wish to tender thanks, a special debt must first be acknowledged to André Mathiot, Maxime Perrin and Lucien de Sainte-Lorette, the respective directors of the *Institut d'études politiques* at Grenoble, the *École des hautes études commerciales* and the *Collège libre des sciences sociales et économiques*; to Fathers d'Ouince, Villain and le Blond, S.J., and to Emile Gabel and Antoine Wenger, editors of the review *Les Études* and the newspaper *La Croix* respectively. By asking me to undertake courses on the Middle East and by supplying me regularly with information on its affairs over the last eight years, these men stimulated the reflections from which this book has emerged.

I feel compelled to record my gratitude and respect for all that I derived from the stimulating and peerlessly perceptive works of my late master, Robert Montagne, who introduced me to the very soil of the Middle East. I wish also to acknowledge my indebtedness to the original work, books and articles of Elizabeth Monroe, Simone and Lean Lacouture, General Georges Catroux, J.-J. Berreby, Marcel Colombe, Elie Kedourie, A. H. Hourani, J. C. Hurewitz, Vincent Monteil, Edouard Sablier and Benjamin Shwadran; and generally to the following periodicals: *l'Afrique et l'Asie* (Paris), *Middle Eastern Affairs* (New York), *l'Orient* (Paris), *Politique étrangère* (Paris), *The World Today* (London), and the daily papers *Le Monde* (Paris) and *L'Orient* (Beirut). Two recent and excellent small works have specially prompted me to write my own: *Die arabische Welt* by Hans Roehrig (Francke Verlag, Berlin, 1955) and *Middle East Crisis* by Guy Wint and Peter Calvocoressi (Penguin Books, Harmondsworth, 1957).

Finally, I have constantly used those indispensable documents for the study of the modern Middle East: *Cahiers de l'Orient contemporain* (Paris), various publications of the *Documentation française* (Paris), *The Middle East* (Chatham House, London), *Oriente Moderno* (Instituto per l'Oriente, Rome) and the compilations of C.H.E.A.M. (Centre de hautes études administratives sur l'Afrique et l'Asie moderne, formerly Centre de hautes études d'administration musulmane.)

* * *

My purpose has been to bring together, in a volume of moderate size and in as assimilable a form as possible, the essential ingredients for serious study of the upheavals in the Middle East today. I have been less concerned to collect facts than to pick out the trends and main stages of an evolutionary process. In pursuing this design I have had to pick and choose in ways that are undoubtedly open to question and which have often gone against the grain; much valuable material has been sacrificed on the grounds that it was only of secondary importance in a general conspectus and in order to concentrate on matters which were more characteristic or in greater need of elucidation. Further, the arrangement of the selected material round central ideas has often involved a sacrifice of chronological order; therefore a list of principal dates is given in an appendix as a help to the reader.

This book is not a compendium but a modest guide. It does not aspire to do more than Ariadne's thread in a Middle Eastern maze which is disconcerting and even perilous but which we may no longer choose to ignore.

PIERRE RONDOT

INTRODUCTION

By Elizabeth Monroe

FOR FORTY YEARS – a classic span in the lands of the Bible – the British prided themselves on paramountcy in the Middle East, and for thirty of those years the pride was justifiable. For instance, the rulers of the Arab states liked and trusted their British friends enough to refrain from embarrassing them on the outbreak of the second World War.

Force of habit is a powerful agent, and for the last of our four decades – the years 1946 to 1956 – most British statesmen and other observers of the scene continued to think in the habitual groove, and so underrated the developments in Arab thinking that were diminishing their one time primacy.

So far, few writers have stepped back and taken a look at those years. Colonel Rondot has now done this. He is of rare breed, for during the bitter years of Anglo-French rivalry in the Levant dispassionate French critics did not exist. But perspective is now available, and he has acquired and offers it from a non-English angle.

In the preface to his French edition, he tells of his introduction to the subject of which he is now a master. As a child, he loved maps, and was given a map of the Balkans and an outfit of coloured pins with which to mark the progress of the armies in the First Balkan war. Naturally, he was on the Christian side, and blue for the Greeks was his favourite. The very names stirred him – Janina, Kirk Kilisse, Chataldja. Suddenly – the date is July 1913 – the quarrel over the spoils began and the pins became all mixed up. Grown-ups tried comfort: 'What do you expect? It's the Eastern Question. It's difficult to understand.' He dates from that moment his interest in the succession to the Ottoman empire.

Just as economists now say that there is a cycle of growth that is the same for all countries, so the student of politics can point to a political cycle. In Latin America in the nineteenth century, in the Balkans yesterday, in the Middle East today and without doubt in Africa tomorrow, the removal or withdrawal of the firm hand of foreign empire leads not to the unity that reigned when all disliked a common master, but to splits of opinion and to quarrels. In both the economic and the political cycles, the unpredictable element is the time taken over each successive stage.

How long will the present stage last in the Middle East? Colonel Rondot is not only a student of Arab affairs, a scholar and a dispassionate observer; just as precious an asset, he is a practised teacher. He sets out in this book to unravel a tangle and provide the layman with a survey not so much of the detail, but of the trends that have determined the decline of Western – principally British – influence, and to describe the current substitutes for it. The explanation leads him into simplification, without over-simplification, of complex topics – where to look for the development of Arab nationalism, how to assess the importance of the Palestine grievance, whether, after 1955, the successful return of Russia into the fray amounts to a mere substitution of new lamps for old. His object, he says, is to single out the main threads in the story, and to embroider only when necessary with 'ancillary but characteristic topics'. This may sound ambitious, but the result of his efforts is the best introduction so far published to the pattern of power in the Middle East. It has been well worth translating because it provides the English-speaking reader with, as it were, the pack of cards which he must know before he can begin to deal them face upwards, and use them for studying the events of every day, let alone the future.

PART I

THE CRISIS OF 1958

Chapter 1

July days

On july 16th, 1958, the Americans were at last stung into action in the Middle East and took a stand in the name of the Western World, whose conscience, brain and strong right arm they claimed to be.

For several months an exceptionally serious crisis had been in full swing. Its course, tortuous and sometimes dramatic, suggested every kind of danger. But the Americans, who had stopped the British and French from marching to Cairo in 1956, had been extremely reluctant to incur in their turn the stigma of intervention. A single dramatic incident forced them to a decision – the assassination of King Feisal of Iraq, his Prime Minister and the heir to the throne, the bloody inauguration of a republic in Baghdad.

This act confronted the Americans with the problem whether to remain indifferent to an appeal for help made to them by President Chamoun of Lebanon. Was he too to be left to be murdered? If so, the West was bound to reap dishonour and ridicule for feebly leaving its adherents to their fate. A few hours later, the British were presented with a similar moral problem in the shape of an appeal from King Hussein of Jordan, and solved it in the same way.

The dice were cast. Events moved forward as relentlessly as if driven by some monster machine. Step by step military plans, long prepared to the smallest detail, were transmuted into a sequence of operations which set down two perfectly equipped forces on Arab soil in a matter of hours. This chain of events created two outstanding impressions, one of implacable power and the other of an irreversible process – a modern version of classic fatalism. At sight of it, friends and enemies, and even the indifferent and the sceptical, were equally struck. Indeed, the whole proceedings conjured up the image of a well-oiled machine serving the purpose of its masters with faultless precision as it ejected silent disciplined soldiers, efficient drivers and mechanics and unruffled troops to camp on Arab soil in the midst of their extraordinarily lavish modern gear. The West could scarcely have bettered this parade of its talents for the benefit of a wondering Orient.

Yet a mere matter of days was enough to show that July 16th, 1958, was not to mark an epoch in the Middle East. Not because the Western machine ran down, nor because its masters were attacked by qualms of conscience, nor because the Russians gave the signal to clear decks for action. There was no wavering in Washington or London, and Moscow held itself in reserve for subtler moves. But the Western gesture had been to some extent made in a vacuum : it did not affect or impinge upon the real issues in the Arab world. The deeper currents flowed unchanged and unchecked round the tiny islets which the West was maintaining as closely guarded reserves for two chiefs of state. Around and about them, disorderly Arab tides eddied and swirled, wholly unaffected.

The days when force could be used to good effect are over, as are the days when a show of might could do service in place of force. There are cases in which force is of no avail. It can compel men's bodies but not their minds; and at some point it becomes a boomerang. The Anglo-Saxon press was quick to realize this, and to see that any solution imposed by British and American arms would be valueless and would merely create unanimous opposition to any proposition whatsoever. The troops had barely reached their destinations before London and New York were wondering how and when to withdraw them again without fatally compromising the régimes that they were meant to be supporting. In any case the intervention was only a single element in a complex scene. It might serve its turn, but only as one piece in a vast puzzle.

Traditional and classic weapons are no longer a respectable

ultima ratio. Only the nuclear bomb can claim that honour, but the bomb – even if there were no moral obstacles to its use in the Middle East – would be no more apposite than the wheel that was used to crush the butterfly. Gunboat diplomacy has been outdated for longer than people imagine. Napoleon might well have had the Middle East in mind when he reflected that in the long run the spirit is mightier than the sword.

Disorder in the Middle East concerns and endangers the West for a variety of reasons, but if the West wants to have its say and carry weight in the Middle East it must do more than hit out. The paramount need is for understanding. The difficulties are immense, for even the practised observer now finds himself more bemused than ever before by the local cross-currents, which are enough to make anyone dizzy and disheartened.

The starting point of this book is the situation in the Middle East at the end of July 1958. It attempts to give a quick sketch of the chaos prevailing at that time, limited to the state of affairs within each state and to the principal local forces which domestic conditions and the events of the moment had set in motion. It then attempts to give a more general view, tracing these developments back to their sources and relating them to each other in order to discover, if possible, some clues to the puzzle. This first section amounts, therefore, to a quick look at a series of snapshots.

Lebanon is a natural starting point. It is nearer to the West than any other part of the Middle East, not only geographically but also in human terms, since its inhabitants are of ancient Mediterranean coastal stock and include a large proportion of Christians. It is also the site of the American intervention of 1958. But its political landscape is appallingly complicated, so much so that at first sight anything so simple as a straightforward military landing seems to have little chance of making an effective impact on local affairs.

Lebanon is a high, narrow mountain range overhanging the sea on the borders of the Arab world. From time immemorial nonconformists of all faiths and dissidents from all temporal dominions have used it as a refuge. Within it, they have been constrained to live together and jointly to defend themselves against outside enemies with the result that, in spite of their differences, Christians and Moslems of all sects have been driven by their mutual desire for independence and stability to develop a tolerance which is to be found nowhere else in the Middle East. Their institutions rest on a finely balanced division of public offices and responsibilities between the various communities or socio-religious groups (Maronite, Greek Orthodox and Greek Catholic Christians; Sunni, Shia and Druze Moslems, etc.), and the state has thus become multi-communal and islamo-christian.

Such division and equilibrium are bound to be delicate even in a country like Lebanon which is endowed with a strong national consciousness and solid traditions. Western influences make a special appeal to the country's Christians, while the Moslems feel a sort of extra allegiance to the wider Moslem community immediately beyond their frontiers. The Christians cherish the concept that they form a bridge between East and West; the Moslems regard the presence of Islam, and the offices held by Moslems in independent Lebanon, as a guarantee of their affinity with the Arab world. The loyalties are comparable but their sources and effects are different, and at a time of crisis the differences may get the upper hand. What is more, the political causes of crisis are many and often compete.

Within the country the preservation of the balance has contributed to the survival not only of the socio-political role of the religious communities,[1] but also of the influence of semi-feudal notables and clans. The party system and parliamentary régime have taken hold only formally and partially. Public opinion has not yet outgrown family and cantonal divisions sufficiently for the men at the top to resist the temptation, at election times, to pull fatally easy strings, for which all sorts of justification can be

[1] Islam draws no sharp distinction between the political and religious spheres, and the Christians of the Middle East have been obliged to accept this concept. See the author's *L'Islam et les musulmans d'aujourd'hui*, pp. 65 ff. and *Les Chrétiens d'Orient*, pp. 72 ff.

made, often enough in good faith. Indispensable links with the West must be preserved because this transit country lives on them in the crude material sense, as well as deriving intellectual and cultural sustenance from them; at the same time the interests of the Arab world have to be protected because 'Arab Lebanon' must show solidarity or else it impairs a significant aspect of its unique nature, not to mention its commercial contacts with its hinterland.

After the Suez affair all these sources of discord and disturbance came to a head at the same time. In November 1956, at the height of the Suez crisis, President Chamoun refused to break off relations with Britain and France as the other Arab states had done.[1] He replaced the pro-Arab government of Abdulla al-Yafi by a new cabinet with two pro-Westerners, Sami Solh and Charles Malik, as Prime Minister and Foreign Minister respectively. In March 1957 he enthusiastically subscribed to the Eisenhower Doctrine on American co-operation with the Middle East.

As a result the more pro-Arab elements in Lebanon accused the President of undue subservience to the West, and particularly to the Anglo-Saxons whose personal vassal he was supposed to have been in the past; at the same time, moderate opinion was alarmed lest Lebanon's traditional equipoise between East and West be compromised and its islamo-christian cohesion threatened. On top of these general complaints, personal rivalries complicated the situation and were exacerbated in that the factions hostile to the President were provided with new and better ammunition – welcome because of the approach of a presidential election due at the end of his term in July 1958.

It was thus at a moment when the country's islamo-christian balance, its balancing act between East and West and the home balance between its factions, were all in jeopardy that the Maronite patriarch, His Beatitude Monsignor Méouchi, who was a personal opponent of the President's faction, declared for the opposition, which he thereby prevented from becoming too

[1] Iraq, too, maintained relations with Britain.

exclusively Moslem. It was at the same moment of unbalance that President Chamoun and Sami Solh used, or condoned the use of, government influence in the parliamentary elections of May 1957, and so ensured the formal defeat of the opposition, which was further being criticized for its hostility to the West.

Thereafter the President was credited, plausibly enough, with the intention to use his comfortable parliamentary majority in order to force through an amendment to the constitution which would permit his re-election for a further term. Indeed some, even outside his own faction, saw advantages in such an operation as a means of preserving Lebanon's independence and connections with the West as against Nasser's rising prestige and panarab ambitions. But the opposition sustained its attack and the murder on the night of May 7th–8th of one of its leading members, a Maronite journalist called Nassib Metni, caused it to gather its strength for a combined effort which quickly developed into armed rising.

Although there was no cut and dried rift between the communities, active insurrection was predominantly the work of Moslems – Sunni, Shia and Druze – and developed in a number of local theatres. One was in Basta, Beirut's Moslem quarter, under Saeb Salam; another in Tripoli under Rashid Karamé; a third in Hermil under Sabri Hamadé; a fourth in the Druze Shuf under Kemal Jumblat, a Gandhian and neutralist socialist who was regularly returned to parliament by his quasi-feudal followers in this district, but had been defeated on this occasion by a palpable trick. Aided by the Syrians (certainly morally and, according to official Lebanese sources, also materially), the revolt was denounced in Beirut as a Nasserite plot. Whether Nasser was directly involved or not, his immense prestige undoubtedly animated and sustained any movement calling itself panarab, whether in Lebanon or elsewhere.

The Lebanese government lodged a complaint before the Security Council and secured the despatch of United Nations observers, but it soon began to accuse these of inefficiency, while the government press expressed its doubts about the perspicacity, and even the good faith and competence, of the secretary-general, Dag Hammarskjöld. Although begged to intervene, the United States for some time evaded the issue. Despite their goodwill towards President Chamoun and their desire to maintain every Western position in the Middle East, they were well aware that the problem was not as simple as that, and that the defeat of the rebels would not of itself mend the rifts in a country which could not, by its very nature, survive without the participation of all its socio-religious groups in its public affairs.

No less an event than the assassination of King Feisal II of Iraq was needed to precipitate an American landing, and even then this landing was undertaken as a precautionary measure rather than as intervention in Lebanon's internal affairs. Partly perhaps in order to prevent a consolidation of foreign intervention, the members of the Lebanese parliament finally agreed on July 31st to elect a compromise President in the person of General Fuad Shehab, who had been noteworthy for his impartiality since the beginning of the crisis. But this choice was a mere stepping stone towards solution, not a final settlement of Lebanon's problem.

Iraq, too, was a vital factor in the crisis. Until the last weeks before the explosion of July 1958, Iraq was regarded not only as a staunch ally of the West but as the wisest, not to say the most stable, state in the Middle East. To all who switched on their radios on the morning of that Fourteenth of July the news of the proclamation of a republic came as a surprise. Yet no objective observer of Middle Eastern affairs need have been surprised by the event.

It is true that the government in Baghdad, profiting from the lavish payments made by the Iraq Petroleum Company, managed these revenues with remarkable prudence and foresight. It allotted the greater part of them to a Development Board which, with the help of foreign advice, was systematically building up an agricultural and industrial economy capable of prospering without the country's extraordinary, though possibly precarious, wealth from oil. Within a matter of years, Iraq was to be possessed of a sound economy on the basis of great dams regulating the devastating floods of the Tigris and Euphrates, the draining of the marsh areas of lower Mesopotamia, the irrigation of the arid land in the north, the production of hydro-electric power, and the construction of factories for chemicals, fertilizers, wood pulp, textiles and building materials. But this admirable plan did not take sufficient account of Iraq's human, psychological and social components. It would, for instance, take a long time to persuade the shiite peasants of the lower Euphrates that the periodic floods had been stopped once and for all thanks to the government's wisdom and enterprise. On the other hand everybody could see that agricultural improvements, unless accompanied by land reform, would benefit only the big land owners, just as the profits from new industries would, a few salaries apart, go to the owners alone.

But the government, taking the view that it was easier to create public well-being without too much regard for public comment, believed that the country's prosperity would benefit the masses in the long run. It thought time was on its side. For a generation T. E. Lawrence's old companion in arms, Nuri Pasha al-Said, had been running affairs, with a few brief and voluntary retirements from the scene. Thanks to the British he had made Iraq, which was granted its independence in 1932, the prime champion of Arab unity and he was looking forward to securing for it the flattering and profitable role in the Arab world which Prussia had played in the unification of Germany. But he judged that this plan required continued and powerful Anglo-Saxon aid. He was over-slow to perceive that the masses and the young were too highly charged with nationalist passion to tolerate the kind of compromises that had been acceptable in the past.

Yet there had been no lack of warnings. A succession of rumblings beneath the Hashemite throne had shaken the unstable fabric of Iraqi politics: the military coup of Bakr Sidqi and Hikmat Sulaiman in 1936, the pro-axis rebellion of Rashid Ali in 1941, the popular demonstrations in 1948 against attempts to make a new treaty with London, and the abortive rising in Baghdad in November 1952. The ease with which the last movement was repressed by the police and the army (as yet loyal) increased the confidence of the authorities; thus they failed to grasp in time that the growing resentment of youth and the frustrations of the small opposition parties, deprived by rigged elections (for instance, those of 1954) of all hope of achieving representation by legitimate means, were gradually affecting the officer corps. Unknown to the populace the army, impressed by the Egyptian revolution in the summer of 1952, was increasingly succumbing to the prestige – immense since the autumn of 1956 – of Colonel Nasser.

The Baghdad Pact, concluded in February 1955 largely on the insistence of the Iraqi government, completed the links between Iraq and the Anglo Saxon West. By this alliance Iraq hoped decisively to strengthen its position; but instead it relegated itself to the fringe of panarabism, a movement which, though lacking political outlet of any official kind, was powerful in terms of Arab feeling. During the spring of 1958 signs of serious internal tension multiplied, and several were plain for all to see. The governments of Ali Jawdat el Ayyubi and Abdul Wahhab Mirjan tried tentatively but in vain to improve relations with the actively panarab states and Nuri Pasha, who returned to power on March 31st, 1958, was equally unsuccessful in his effort to give the Development Board a wider national character. The formation, with Jordan, of an Arab Union on February 14th could hardly be taken for anything more than a retort to Nasserism.

In July 1958 the Iraqi plan to send troops to Lebanon to assist the forces of order against the pro-Nasser insurgents provided the 'free officers' with a final motive for a rising which had been prepared and decided on much earlier. The movement was to come to a head in a matter of hours. The leaders wished it to be bloodless and such it would have been if the Baghdad mob, heady with suppressed exasperation, had not murdered the Crown Prince and former regent, Abdul Illah, and the Prime

Minister, Nuri al-Said – the men responsible for repressing the revolt of 1941, for the British alliance and the Baghdad Pact. King Feisal II, though too young to have incurred any personal responsibility, was also murdered in the chaos of the first few moments.

These excesses revealed the violence of popular Arab passions. But the members of the new Iraqi government, which had tried to prevent and at least managed to curb them, were not among the actual perpetrators. The President of the Sovereignty Council, Major General Nazib al-Rubai, and the Prime Minister, Brigadier Abdul Karim Kassem, were enlightened and patriotic officers who had studied their profession in England. Their immediate concern was to avoid upsets, and one of their first acts was to calm foreign residents, many of them connected with Iraq's major public works and with the Iraq Petroleum Company, dispenser of the vital royalties. Although they dissolved the Arab Union with Jordan, they showed no desire to amalgamate Iraq with Nasser's United Arab Republic, nor even to establish a federal link with it as Yemen had done. After a long fever the Iraqi abscess had burst, and the next step was for the country to find its feet again under the guidance of a truly national government.

CHAPTER 2

Nasser's ambitions and the Northern Tier

IN 1958 THE THREE other Middle Eastern members of the Baghdad Pact – Iran, Turkey and Pakistan – were less in the public eye than Iraq. Pakistan lies outside the area covered by this book but Iran and Turkey belong at heart to the Middle East, in spite of certain appearances, and must come into any survey of its crisis.

Of all the eastern members of the Baghdad Pact, Iran seemed the least committed to its alignments. During the summer of 1956 the Shah paid an official visit to the U.S.S.R., the first sovereign to do so; meanwhile, the Americans were pouring military help into his country, aid which he was at pains to describe as purely defensive. In the spring of 1958 he paid a private visit to the United States and, significantly, made a detour in order to visit Japan. These trips symbolize a determined effort to strike some advantageous balance, a policy facilitated by the fact that Iran went through its major national crisis earlier than the Arab States and, as it were, in a vacuum.

It was in 1951 that the Mossadeq government, hoping to get the Anglo-Iranian Oil Company to agree to the magic 50-50 formula for the division of oil royalties, nationalized its oil reserves. But its western customers were easily able to dispense with Iranian oil because the other Middle Eastern countries – Iraq, Saudi Arabia and Kuwait – far from showing solidarity, stepped up their production of crude oil to replace Iran's. In 1954 a compromise was reached. Mossadeq disappeared and the oil-fields remained nationalized, but a consortium of foreigners leased them from the Iranian National Oil Company. Britain, deprived of its monopoly, was joined by American and French colleagues, and later Japanese and Italian rivals offering even more seductive terms.

Whereas the U.S.S.R. never put decisive pressure on Iran, it had constantly made its power felt. The Russians may have thought that so long as Iran remained relatively weak, socially and strategically, it was preferable as a western ally than as a burdensome Soviet satellite, or a too canny neutral. Might not Iran, so large and difficult to defend, constitute the soft underbelly of the Baghdad Pact? But no matter what the Russians thought, when violent crisis shook Iraq, Iran's only reaction was a demand that the pact be strengthened – in other words, for more aid. Its foreign policy remained and remains equivocal, no doubt deliberately so. It could be more vigorous if the country had a more solid internal balance. The monarch himself certainly appreciates the need for more social justice, a fairer distribution of land and wealth and a closer association of the people with public affairs. But he never seems able to carry with him the traditional ruling class, which claims to be the backbone of the country and opposes all major reforms.

Turkey's approach to its problem was different. Fears prompted by the very nearness of the U.S.S.R. (particularly after 1945 when Russia showed signs of wishing to challenge Turkey's territorial integrity, the status of the Straits and the non-democratic régime in Ankara) drove it into the arms of the West, in particular of the United States, from which it set out to get all it could in the way of assistance and support. As a recipient of Truman aid from 1947, a member of Nato from February 1952 after insistent requests to join, and as prime mover, with Iraq, in the creation of the Baghdad Pact in the winter of 1955, Turkey was an insatiable applicant for American aid in all its forms. Thanks to this help, never regarded as adequate in Ankara, it steadily increased its general, industrial and strategic resources and gradually equipped itself for the leading political role which it hoped to play in the Middle East.

Thus Turkey was in the throes of crisis, but such a crisis was due to its own plethora and ambition. From the heroic period of the Kemalist reform (1920–23) extended, under the Popular Republican party (1938–50), Turkey under the Democratic Party (in power from May 1950) preserved its national momentum intact; it also preserved something of its laicism, but nothing at all of the strict autarchy or the prudent husbandry of its Anatolian fastness. Financial and trade crises, soon chronic, were staved off by American aid since there could, for the west, be no question of abandoning such an irreplaceable bastion. In return for this help, Turkey acted as spearhead for all the West's plans for the defence of the Middle East, whether the Middle East Defence Organization (1951) or the Baghdad Pact (1955). At such times it showed a mounting degree of willingness to put political pressure on the Arab states; Syria, for instance, could hardly fail to be influenced by Turkey's military superiority.

As Nato's easternmost member, Turkey sometimes seemed over-ready to commit the Western coalition – to be too bold a vanguard. Valued in Washington for its unflinching anti-Russian stand, Ankara exercised considerable influence on the Middle Eastern policies of the United States. Last but not least, Turkey was the only appreciable military power in the Middle East. Altogether these circumstances endowed Turkey with a dangerous capacity to exacerbate Arab concerns. And Turkish growing pains played an indirect, though considerable, role in the events of the summer of 1958, notably in the delicate problem of Cyprus.

A Mediterranean island, four-fifths Greek and one-fifth Turkish in population, Cyprus is an indifferent naval base but an excellent aircraft carrier on the edge of the Arab world. Pledged to Great Britain in 1878 by the Ottoman empire and converted into a Crown Colony in 1914, its natural fate would have been union with the kingdom of Greece, as happened in 1945 to Rhodes and the Dodecanese with their similar racial composition and histories. But the forcible and swift abandonment of British political and military positions in the Middle East immediately after the second World War gave Cyprus added value in British eyes and Britain was loath to give it up.

London, as though instinctively pursuing the old formula of 'divide and rule', had tried to counter Greek claims by encouraging Turkish minority pretensions, soon enthusiastically adopted by the government in Ankara. And so there developed, year in, year out, a long struggle in the course of which the Greek population turned to guerilla warfare and terrorism. Turkey proposed a partition which would give it the island's northern coast; the Greek Cypriots, encouraged by mainland Greeks and backed to some extent by the Greek government, demanded *enosis* – that is, union with Greece – or the independence which would allow them to bring this about. The sympathies of the Arab peoples lay with the Greek Cypriots, because Cyprus was the base in Western hands which made possible the Anglo-French attack on the Suez canal in the autumn of 1956, and because Greece had always refused to recognize the state of Israel. So, paradoxically, Nasser lent the support of his prestige to people of Greek blood and Christian faith who were at loggerheads with a Moslem Turkish minority over the liberation of their island.

Each local aspect of the crisis in the Middle East leads in a bee-line to the master of Egypt. Cairo's role should now be defined.

Incontestably the eye of the Arab hurricane, Egypt, appropriately, seems calm. From Cairo Nasser's prestige radiates to the Arab countries and even, as Cyprus shows, to the whole of the Middle East. Yesterday's *bikbashi*[1] is today President of the United Arab Republic which embraces Egypt and Syria as 'provinces' and is linked with the Yemen. But Nasser's official position represents only a small part of his true power: to the vast majority of the Arabs, from the populous cities of the Levant to the villages of Mesopotamia and the oases of the Arab Peninsula, he is the Master, the supreme hero and undoubted chief.

Western opinion, which likes to think itself objective, is slow to appreciate the depth and potency of the Nasser legend, the mainsprings of which it failed to perceive. Gamal Abdel Nasser

[1] A military term of Turkish origin: 'chief of a thousand', the equivalent of lieutenant-colonel.

was not the leader of the Egyptian officers who, heartbroken and horrified by Israel's victory in 1948, drove out inefficient and unworthy rulers and seized their power for the good of the people and the state, as Husni Zaim and Adib Shishakli had done in Syria before them. But the difference between him and them was that he knew, whether by intelligent reasoning, or by sound intuition akin to political sense, how to keep the reins in his hands. He eliminated not only the fanatical activists of the Moslem brotherhood, most of his original comrades in the struggle, and the corrupt politicians who had weathered more than one national storm, but also his senior, the wise General Neguib.

Nasser was by no means the first person in Egypt to contend against the 'unequal treaties' which sanctioned and confirmed foreign intervention and influence. Unlike the Wafd in 1951, he did not resort to guerilla activities against the British. But it was he who negotiated and, in August 1954, secured the evacuation of the Suez canal base – a process to be completed in June 1956.

At times, his foreign policy had its failures. While on the one hand he carried the blockade of Israel to the illegal limit of closing the Suez canal to Israeli traffic, he proved unable, prior to the clash of 1956, to bring the Palestine problem any nearer solution. Nor did he manage to extend the Egyptian dominion of his dreams to Libya, or to the Sudan, which had been all but won over by Neguib. The United States agreed to give him aid, as to any applicant; but it was Iraq that the West endowed with the greater benefits. Not until much later, and then only sparingly, did the U.S.S.R. vouchsafe him the long-term credits for the economically vital high dam at Aswan – credits in the hope of which he had procrastinated with the Americans. But thanks to an exceptional gift for changing direction he always succeeded in masking his defeats and overlaying them with acts which stuck in the Arab mind to the exclusion of all else. Although disappointed by his nearest neighbours in Africa, he captivated a large part of Western Asia. Paralysed by the West's restrictive practices – its insistence on the maintenance of the *status quo* in the Middle East, and on limiting the provision of Western arms and credits – he turned to Russia. The unrestricted supply of Czech and Russian arms from September 1955 was an outstanding triumph which enabled Egypt to counterbalance Iraq, the Western favourite, to become a major menace to Israel, and to reassume the heroic role of leader of the Arabs against their common enemy.

In the same way, Nasser glossed over the check to his hopes of building the Aswan high dam by proclaiming the nationalization of the Suez canal. Again, though his troops were routed in Sinai by the Israelis and driven out of Port Said by the English and French, not only did he transform military disaster into a grand-scale diplomatic triumph by getting the United Nations, the United States and the U.S.S.R. to force Great Britain, France and Israel to suspend operations and retreat from Egyptian soil; he also suceeded through adroit propaganda in turning his military defeat into a sensational feat of arms in Arab eyes.

From then on his huge prestige throughout the Middle East steadily increased. Having saved him, the United States could not make up their minds whether to help him as a sincere nationalist or keep him in check as a dictator and their hesitation demonstrated their distrust of him. His socio-economic projects, such as agrarian reform and the development of the Liberation Province, have come to a halt, but only the West has interpreted these failures as a weakness of the régime. The Arabs, so far as they have noticed them at all, see in them an added reason for hating imperialism, to which they attribute all such setbacks. The burning zeal of Nasser the reformer, which is wholly sincere, keeps him his good name. To the Arab masses, he is not only the Bismarck who will unite them, but also, because of his ambitious social programme and his effective hostility to foreign-aided and conservative régimes, a kind of Garibaldi. Pockets of resistance continue to exist in plenty and, as we shall see, Arab rivalries are far from being resolved; but in the eyes of the majority Nasser's star is still in the ascendant, heralding a bright future.

Nasser's prestige is greater outside the U.A.R., where only his services to the Arab cause are seen, than in his own country; the majority is dazzled by these exploits but there are others in all strata of society who are aware of certain facts. For instance, the memory of the military flight from Sinai and the great fear prevailing in Cairo at the beginning of November 1956 prevent some people (however few they may be) from swallowing the story of his invincibility. Then too the precariousness and inadequacy of the Egyptian economy is evident in spite of various kinds of help and of partial successes, including the unfreezing of balances held in Washington and London, the agreement with the old Suez Canal Company, limited technical and financial co-operation with the United States, Great Britain and the U.S.S.R., good economic relations with Germany, France, etc., and the normal and profitable working of the Suez canal. The Egyptian economy depends on cotton, which is not always easy to sell and for ever threatened by competition, owing to the lack of stored water (and consequently land left untilled and a shortage of hydro-electric power) the Egyptians cannot exploit their vast potentialities for the production of cheap cotton on a scale which could give them almost a world monopoly. Neither can they increase their production of foodstuffs, nor develop their industry in order to guarantee an adequate and stable standard of living for their steadily increasing population. The real solution is the construction of the Aswan dam, a project which cannot materialize for many years to come. Improvement of the Suez canal, a less ambitious but none the less grandiose plan, is more within Egyptian capacities; it would give Egypt a decisive role in the oil transit business and a greatly increased income, although this income would still not be enough to solve its social and economic problems. In any case the goal is a distant one. As for agrarian reform, here as elsewhere it has only reached a very early stage and its value is mainly psychological. Thus Egypt's socio-economic crisis remains dormant.

In the political field the situation is healthier. The opposition (Wafd, monarchists, Moslem Brotherhood, Left extremists) has been either crushed or silenced. Those who remain secret opponents, although not insignificant in numbers, are powerless; the social and economic uncertainty works in their favour, but Nasser's successes abroad (which have not yet been surveyed in full) cut much of the ground from under their feet. So long as Nasser makes disciples in Baghdad, asserts himself in Damascus, worries Washington, counts in Moscow, interests Belgrade and Peking and causes headaches in London and Paris, it would be naïve to suppose that he could successfully be defied in Cairo.

The best example of Nasser's potency is Syria, in theory equal to Egypt but manifestly in second place, a province of the United Arab Republic created at the beginning of 1958 under his presidency. This union of Syria with Egypt seems to have been the first event which, however belatedly, opened the eyes of the West to the Egyptian dictator's magnetic attraction for the Arabs.

Although nationalist and independent at heart, Syria sacrificed its rightful integrity at the beginning of 1958 in the cause of Arab unity under the spur of an overmastering panarab enthusiasm and under the leadership of a gifted and quick-witted *élite*. It will be easier to understand this astonishing sacrifice and to estimate its future effect and prospects, after first sketching the contemporary balance of forces in the Middle East, and retracing recent political developments in terms of certain dominant themes.

This political scuttling act was only one point in a long and overt Syrian crisis which reflected in various forms the country's basic character. On February 28th, 1954, Syria reverted to a parliamentary régime after five years of paternalism under military dictatorship; but although this régime was able to operate more equitably than anywhere else in the Arab Middle East thanks to Syria's maturer political development and education, the free play of parties and opinion could not provide a solution for the country's most urgent political problems.

Syria suffered from a chronic feeling of isolation which assumed the proportions of a pathological obsession in the last months of its independent existence. It felt itself set apart owing to historic memories of Damascus as the ancient capital of the Omayyads and to cultural influences (even briefly that of the French mandate) which helped to form its republican spirit. Yet it was too deeply ensconced in the Moslem Arab world to feel at one with Lebanon, whose whole purpose was to serve as a link between East and West. It therefore saw itself as hedged about by hostility and distrust – Turkey's surly attitude; the alliance of the Hashemite monarchies of Iraq and Transjordan (subsequently Jordan) with their ambition to create a unified 'fertile crescent' dominated by Baghdad; the Iraqi-Turkish coalition in the Baghdad Pact; the danger of Zionism, later of Israel, with its outposts less than an hour's car drive from the Syrian capital; and finally the constellation of the Eisenhower Doctrine, to which all the surrounding states in one way or another subscribed. Suspicious of American aid, perhaps exaggeratedly so (General Shishakli himself refused Point Four aid), Syria in its isolation took the equally extreme step of seeking aid exclusively from the Russians, with the result that by the summer of 1957 the extent of this aid had awakened in its neighbours, and even in the United States, an open distrust which further irritated Syrian susceptibilities.

A solidly united state could easily have faced up to these tensions and pressures, but Syria was an amalgam containing a set of individualistic local nationalisms (especially strong in Damascus), the Baath's socialism (anti-communist but intent upon Arab unity), a pro-Iraqi people's party with an essentially economic basis (especially strong in Aleppo), an army propelled into politics by patriotism and bewitched by Nasser's prestige, conservatives aghast at the vigour of the Left and the preponderance of Soviet aid, pseudo-fascist activities, utopian Moslems, and trouble-shooting opportunists of the extreme Left.

In order to understand how all these various streams could suddenly be brought to join forces in an enthusiastic mass rally under the aegis of Nasser one day in the winter of 1957, we have to look into the sources of the movement for Arab unity and the ancillary reasons for its strength at that moment. But it must be noted at the outset that in spite of the prestige of Nasser's name, the integration of Syria with Egypt has proved a laborious undertaking. It has shown signs of stress not only on the political level (where persistent Syrian individualism has provoked grave internal quarrels and strained to breaking point the tempers of none too tactful Egyptian officials) but above all in the economic field. Here there is such disparity of interest that the Cairo authorities themselves seemed to hesitate to implement a union which ran counter to the nature of things and to the customary course of business interests. So the fever in Syria did not abate. The help given by the United Arab Republic to the Lebanese revolt should probably be credited to the Syrian side of the partnership, particularly to the Baath socialists and senior army officers; everything goes to show that Nasser was afraid the venture was risky and premature, and only agreed to it under the pressure of Syrian impatience.

The events of July 1958 brought two new elements into play which might in theory have been expected to deflate Syria's chronic crisis but which give every appearance of further complicating it in the long run. On the one hand the Hashemite monarchy in Baghdad collapsed; on the other a compromise was reached in Beirut. Thus the vice in which Syria, rightly or wrongly, had felt itself gripped, was relaxed on two sides. Logically, this should have reduced the feeling of compulsion to link with Egypt; and straight away, mingled with rejoicing over Baghdad and repining over Beirut, voices were raised in Damascus in favour of a more federal and less unitary framework for Arab unity and a geographically wider Arab union than the existing United Arab Republic. But could the complex of Syria be reduced to such simple terms, and could Nasser give a freer hand so soon to a province which had already proved over-recalcitrant? At the time, to Cairo as to Washington and London, Syria was not the only country which called urgently for attention: there were also Jordan and the territories on the periphery of Arabia, the bastions of a Middle Eastern policy to which Britain still clung.

Chapter 3

Modern Israel and the last of the Arab kingdoms

The junior partner of Iraq in the Anglo-Hashemite game in the Middle East, and although weaker and seemingly more menaced, the Jordanian monarchy nevertheless survived the Iraqi monarchy in July 1958. But whereas Iraq seemed to find a new balance as a republic, Jordan remained unstable and inflammable; there is a danger that the first serious setback will not only destroy the régime but also cause the state to disintegrate and the country to disappear.

The little half-bedouin emirate of Transjordan, which gradually achieved autonomy under Britain's tactful guidance, became the Kingdom of Jordan in 1948. From the Palestine disaster it gained new territory but with it an increase of population consisting of the peasant and middle-class inhabitants of Cisjordania (Jerusalem, Hebron, Nablus and Samaria) and also more than 500,000 Arab refugees who fled from the territories which became the State of Israel.

These events substantially altered Jordan's attitude and political balance: against the Hashemite monarchy was pitted the influence of Nasser. At first the throne compromised; it had been rudely forewarned by disorders such as those which broke out during a visit by General Templer, Chief of the British Imperial General Staff, in the autumn of 1955. In May 1956 King Hussein dismissed the most far-seeing of his British counsellors and mentors, General Glubb; after the pro-Nasser elections of October 21st, 1956, he entered into a military alliance with Egypt and Syria; finally he dispensed with the subsidies from the British, who evacuated the air bases which they still held in the country.

After the Suez crisis, however, King Hussein took the first

opportunity to extricate himself from the combined pressures of internal and external Arab nationalism. In April 1957, with the help of Saudi Arabian forces sent by the neighbouring sovereign and with the virtual support of the American Sixth Fleet at anchor in Eastern Mediterranean waters, he dissolved the pro-Nasser parliament and appointed a 'moderate' ministry loyal to himself. This new Jordanian government never relaxed vigilance on its frontier with Israel (the most active section of Israel's borders since a U.N. force had become responsible for patrolling the demarcation line in Sinai); yet it lost the goodwill and support of Egypt and its satellites. When Arab payments, which were to have replaced the British subsidies, were only partially honoured and then stopped altogether, Jordan at once turned to the British exchequer, at the same time continuing to receive American aid for the ephemeral and precarious national economy.

Having thus returned, albeit informally, to the Ango-Saxon orbit, the throne and the government in Amman set out to check Nasser's ambitions. In this they had the support of the army, the police and the Transjordan section of the population but the strenuous opposition of the Palestinian majority. To the formation of the United Arab Republic by the Egyptian dictator, they replied by forming, on February 14th, 1958, a Hashemite confederation with Iraq under the title of the Arab Union.

The assassination at Baghdad on July 14th, 1958, of the President of this Union, King Feisal of Iraq, and his Prime Minister Nuri al-Said, caused a grave crisis at Amman. The dramatic death of his cousin made King Hussein, nominally at least, the head of the Union, and he toyed briefly with the idea of reconquering Iraq in the name of the Federation. Then, judging that he too ran the risk of meeting with a tragic end, he asked for protection from Great Britain, which landed a parachute brigade on Amman airport on July 16th. The exceptional nature of this step, and the fact that, though solicited by the legitimate Jordanian authorities, it was secretly strongly condemned by a very great part of public opinion, reveal the acuteness of the Jordan crisis. In a Middle East swayed by Nasser, Jordan was in theory a Western strongpoint, even an arsenal; in fact, it was a highly exposed outpost and many people, even in the Anglo-Saxon world, believed that by using force to retain it, the British were running the risk of weakening and complicating their position rather than taking effective action.

In spite of appearances, the other positions held by Great Britain on the eastern edge of the Arabian peninsula appeared less jeopardized. Besides the Crown Colony of Aden, there are a series of territories under petty rulers or local potentates bound to Britain by Advisory Treaties – the Western and Eastern Aden Protectorates (Lahej, Hadramaut, etc.), the sultanate of Muscat, the sheikhdoms of the Trucial Coast (Abu Dhabi, etc.), the island of Bahrein, the emirates of Quatar and Kuwait. The British were first attracted to these coasts by their strategic importance on the route to India, and the strategic consideration continued to hold good when they became useful rear positions on the flank of the Middle East. They acquired further value from the prospect (and in Bahrein, Quatar and Kuwait the reality) of oil production. The emirate of Kuwait, in spite of the meagre area of its sparsely populated territory, is in the front rank of Middle Eastern producers, in some years outclassing even Saudi Arabia.

In different degrees and under various forms these lands are influenced by Arab nationalism. This is inspired increasingly by Nasser, and in helping their rulers to defend themselves the British are protecting their own interests. In some cases, particularly on the south-eastern side of the peninsula, there have been full-scale rebellions, more or less openly supported from outside. Although the Buraimi affair in 1955 was no more than a sharp border dispute started by Saudi Arabia against the sheikh of Abu Dhabi (who was successfully backed by the British), the revolt in Oman in June 1956 challenged the sovereignty of the Sultan of Muscat in an important part of his territory where agents of Cairo were trying to set up an 'independent' ruler. At the end of the same year fighting on the western borders of Aden, begun by rebels who had Yemeni support, was designed to detach the protectorates of that region from the tutelage of London.

These various incidents can be attributed to grandiose schemes thought up in Cairo; but in such archaic countries events still take the traditional forms of a tribal rising or a coup by a clan, and there Britain's old Middle East hands, reinforced by smallish detachments of the R.A.F., have found the last theatre where effective use can be made of their experience and *savoir faire*. At the beginning of the summer of 1958 the excitement seemed to have died down throughout these peripheral territories. The trouble persisting in one of them, the sultanate of Lahej, brought on July 10th a British reaction in the purest colonial style – the deposition of the sultan – and in spite of a few protests the method worked. Even in certain British circles, however, it is not thought that such means can be indefinitely used.

In the little territories on the north-eastern side of the peninsula, with the possible exception of the Trucial Coast, the face of things has changed already. Quatar, Bahrein and above all Kuwait, more open to Western influence and penetration than the mountainous areas in the south, have been prospected with such success that oil production has become the only thing that counts, politically and socially as well as economically. Through modern industrial and financial techniques London has strengthened the links forged long ago with these minor rulers. In receipt of fabulous royalties, these leave the city to administer the wealth which neither their extravagance nor their liberality can exhaust; thus, a ruler of Kuwait finds it easy to resist Cairo's temptingly whispered invitation to turn his little state into the 'banker brother' of the Arab League or of some new federation, while his generous paternalism makes the government of his subjects relatively easy. But such structures have their weaknesses and the first signs of these are visible. An Arab proletariat is beginning to take shape, on a small scale but susceptible to various subversive forces, and public opinion is awakening (inspired of course by Nasser) while the semimonopoly of the British oil companies and their associates is threatened by the bids of rivals such as the Japanese.

When parachutists were sent to Amman on July 16th, 1958, London may have been under the impression that it was taking preventive action to defend Kuwait and, more immediately, Aden. There were grounds for this belief, but the order of priorities may well have been faulty.

The presence in the peninsula of two major states, Saudi Arabia and Yemen, is understandably important to the smaller peripheral territories. In the past the natural geographical barriers of mountain and desert have had to be reinforced by diplomatic means: between Kuwait and Saudi Arabia, for example, a neutral zone was created which in its turn became the subject of bids by oil companies.

Saudia Arabia and Yemen have been overtaken by the times while still sunk in the traditional stability of mediaeval institutions, represented in the one case by puritanical Wahhabism and in the other by a Zeidi imamate. Their reactions, although different, have served to protect both their sovereigns from the critical effects of the modernization of the Middle East; and, provisionally at any rate, conservatism has been moderately successful.

In Saudi Arabia King Abd el Aziz ibn Saud and his successor King Saud ibn Abd el Aziz have avoided being caught, as certain Western observers expected them to be caught, between the alternatives of Ford or Gandhi; but up to a point they have tried to be both. Thus the Saudi Arabian monarch borrowed such Western techniques as cars and radio telegraphy to control the steppes and the nomads, and the exploitation of oil to improve his finances. At the same time he rejected the Western outlook and continued to subject his people to a harsh traditional way of life from which only he himself, his family and his senior officials were exempt. The huge revenues from the oil concessions granted to American companies increased both his power and his luxurious pomp without in any way lessening his despotic claims or the severity of his rule. He hoped to garner Western stipends as well as Moslem prestige, and the Americans were content to play his game. When the Eisenhower Doctrine was proclaimed they welcomed him in Washington with unwonted attentions and sought to make him the protagonist of American policy and, in spite of the mediaeval character of his rule, a sort of trustee for the West in the Middle East.

But although Saudi Arabian policy in Arab affairs had always been elastic (even over Palestine there were more declarations of principle and taking up of attitudes than action), the Saudis either could not or would not stick to the consequences of endorsing the Eisenhower Doctrine. In the spring of 1957 Saudi Arabia gave effective help in rescuing the Jordanian dynasty; yet in the summer of the same year it remained inactive when the United States hoped for its mediation in Syria – a step which the government in Damascus quickly decided to be unwanted.

This trend continued in spite of occasional variations and by the autumn of 1958 even adherence to the Eisenhower Doctrine had been for practical purposes repudiated. In the following spring, although Riyadh congratulated Baghdad but not Cairo on its work for Arab unity, and although loud complaints were heard in Damascus about a Saudi Arabian plot against the new President of the United Arab Republic, King Saud immediately made a move in Nasser's direction by formally conferring on his reputedly pro-Nasser brother, the emir Feisal, powers which the emir had long possessed in form but not in fact. Further, the king made a great show of removing a number of 'evil' Syrian and Palestinian advisers.

This palace revolution was probably less important than some Western observers imagined. The king's personal power was in no way infringed, while the solidarity of the dynasty was probably reinforced. In any case Saudi Arabian external policy remained cautious and reserved, as subsequent events in Lebanon, Iraq and Jordan were to show. But the Americans who looked to Saudi Arabia for significant support in the Middle East were wholly disappointed.

Was the threat of an internal crisis one of the unknown factors which influenced King Saud? In Saudi Arabia the people have benefited even less from oil profits than in Iraq, where the royalties have at least contributed to the economy of the country if not to its social well-being. In Saudi Arabia the money has been almost exclusively appropriated to purchasing influence abroad (if not to straight corruption) and to meeting the expenses of the king, the princes and their favourites; and the scale of these demands is such that the exchequer has frequently been empty or even in debt. Signs of ferment have at times been noticeable among the workers in the oil-fields of the east coast, and the bourgeoisie of the Hedjaz has displayed ill-humours which may have been shared by certain princes, including the emir Feisal. But each of these classes was too small, the authority of the sovereign over the tribes too widespread, and the power of the machinery of government too great for such movements to be more than warning signs. Meanwhile Nasser's ceaseless propaganda grinds on and the calm of Saudi Arabia is probably more apparent than real.

In Yemen an equally antiquated structure gives the same appearance of internal stability. Here, however, we have to bear in mind the proximity of Aden, the temptations offered to an ambitious imam by the 'irredentist' territories of the protectorates, and the impression that British demonstrations can make on the Yemeni authorities. The zeidi imamate, based on divine right, has taken care to keep Yemen as far removed as possible from contemporary influences and, unlike Saudi Arabia, has even rejected Western techniques. All the same the dynasty has not escaped upheavals, sometimes bloody ones. The imam Yahya was assassinated in February 1948 and dissident princes and notables, describing themselves as 'free Yemenis', have frequently had support from the not disinterested British in Aden. The claims of Yemen against the Western Aden Protectorate and the fighting which took place on the frontier at the beginning of 1958 have already been mentioned. Upon the creation on March 8th, 1958, of the United Arab Federation, consisting of the United Arab Republic and Yemen, the latter had all the appearance of a Nasserite outpost facing the British bastion at Aden, but there followed no appreciable increase of Yemeni belligerence.

There remains Israel, planted on the Mediterranean verge of the Arab world like a barb in its flesh. Israel, itself in an almost continual state of internal crises, injects a powerful element of crisis into the affairs of its neighbours. Drawing as it does on the material and emotional reserves of world jewry, it is bound to react to moods in the diaspora which are often at variance with its own.

At the end of July 1958, however, Israel's name scarcely figured in the tragic Middle East drama. The crisis of the autumn of 1956, when Israel took up arms against the Egyptians in Sinai (and could have considered itself cheated of victory by the West), ended in an incomplete, precarious but not unfavourable, form of pacification. U.N. forces, strung out between Israelis and Egyptians, effectively froze the demarcation line between the Negev and Sinai, previously the scene of so many explosions; and the same force stationed at Sharm es Sheikh on the straits of Tiran opened the Gulf of Akaba to shipping using Israel's new eastern port of Eilat and breathed fresh life into the Israeli economy from the vast expanses of Asia. Israel now had only one active front – the Jordanian sector from Tiberias to Akaba – for one need scarcely count the Lebanese borders (always fairly quiet) nor even the Syrian sector, short, uneasy, but not active enough to prevent the successful draining of the Huleh marshes.

But Israel's problems were not confined to the demarcation lines – those inflammable reminders of its dramatic and painful injection into a hostile Arab world. It had also to live in a state of semi-blockade, while trying to build up its internal resources by hard work and resourcefulness, and to get vital help from the outside world and from world jewry. This last task involved exacting adjustments, since the spirit of the diaspora, though in general liberal (where it is not religio-conservative), accords ill with the socialist ideology predominating in Israel itself. Within the state, moreover, the socialist team works under difficulties; it wears itself out, or alternatively, becomes rigid when confronted with religious or capitalist objection to its doctrines; at the same time its collective settlements are withering away as the pioneers grow old and bourgeois and the hard facts of life tell against their economic pattern. This is a perennial trouble, passionately discussed among the Israelis themselves but little noticed in the outside world.

The enmity felt for Jordan, on the other hand, is a thing of the moment and too clamorous to be missed – as witness the violent incident on Mount Scopus in the suburbs north of Jerusalem on May 26th, 1958, when the Canadian chief of the U.N. observers was killed. And the British parachutists who established themselves on Amman airport on July 16th, 1958, supported an Arab government unwelcome to Israel although allied to the West. The Israeli government complained that the 'air bridge' from Cyprus to Jordan passed over its territory, and the permission granted to the British to fly over Israel was always unreliable and soon virtually revoked.

At this point we come upon a curious twist in the Middle East crisis, which is a good example of its intricacy. Time and again events have suggested that Israel (unlike so many Western observers and especially the West's Middle Eastern allies and associates) was not so immovably convinced that Nasser's prime destiny and purpose was to make trouble in the Middle East. The circumstances which cushioned or disguised the main causes of friction between Israel and Egypt after the end of 1956 have already been described, but these developments, important though they were, do not entirely explain Israel's attitude to the Nasser legend and its disruptive effects in the Middle East. The calmness with which the Israeli government accepted the creation of the United Arab Republic has already been mentioned, though without finding a fully satisfactory explanation for this attitude. Possibly Israel thinks it may be easier to reach an understanding with a single powerful Arab neighbour, led by a man of enough standing to make his followers accept his decisions (however unpopular), than with a whole pack of enemies competing with and outbidding each other under leaders who, being weak, can retain power only by constantly brandishing the Israeli menace as the source of every evil.

This theory finds some confirmation in the fact that Israel, far from setting itself up as of a different composition from its neighbours, is for ever representing itself as just another Middle Eastern state, thus indicating that it could come to an understanding with the Arabs. It is not Israel but a certain brand of Arab propaganda which has represented the new state as an emanation of the West, a part of Europe monstrously implanted in the Arab East.

In Israel immigration has continuously increased the proportions of 'oriental' Jews (from Yemen, Iraq, Libya and the Maghreb) with the result that the nation has become more truly oriental and more appositely located. Such considerations have not extinguished controversy over the appropriation of territory which the Arabs regard as theirs, but the use to which it has been put has shown a tendency to look for compromise and common ground. There have been other signs that certain Israelis have a sincere desire for negotiation.

It is not yet appropriate to discuss the prospects for the future; but in putting the final touches to this overall sketch of the Middle East in crisis stress must again be laid on the extreme diversity of the elements involved. To conclude: it is impossible to reach an informed and firm opinion about that, or indeed any, Middle East crisis by looking only at the events of the moment. All evidence points to a need to look back, to trace the course of the major forces at work, and to pursue the drama through its earlier stages. Only thus can the essential nature of the problem be appreciated and the way felt to an understanding of its future course. This analysis follows.

PART II

THE BOARD AND THE PIECES

Chapter 1

The inconstant Middle East

First of all, the setting: the chessboard of the Middle East. A swift glance at the map reveals its special features – a complex of vitally important road and water ways separated by natural barriers, together with natural resources which dazzle and tempt the West but which vary in value with the times and so give this part of the world a character of constant flux.

Moreover the use both of the routes and the wealth of the Middle East depends on the men who live there, who can open or bar the way to them, and who have shifted from one mood to another throughout the ages. These men differ greatly in race, tongue and creed, so that the complicated geography of the land is overlaid by a social and national motley which is as fluid as the pattern of material values.

In the last analysis it is the sources of these differences which we must understand. Only then can we attempt to assess the operative forces in the context of our own times: forces for and against change, currents of idealism and expediency, local pressures and the covetousness of the outside world.

The Middle East is the junction of Asia, Africa and Europe. At the vital point where these three ancient continents meet, it presents an extraordinary combination of routes and barriers, an alternation of deep sea inlets and land shelves which man is always trying to master. These geographical features are familiar enough; but too little thought has been given to the tangled yet compact configuration which distinguishes the Middle East from the shapeless masses of Asia Minor and Africa.

The Straits of Constantinople, the Bosphorus and the Dardanelles provide access to the Mediterranean for the regions of the Black Sea and the Caucasus and, more important, for the steppes of Russia and central Europe which are drained by the great rivers Danube, Dnieper and Don. In fact the rivers themselves flow through the straits, as the cold, almost fresh, water of the current demonstrates. Beyond the narrow continental shelf of the Caucasus another vast river and sea system, that of the Caspian and the Volga, is connected to the Mediterranean world. A whole northern world depends on this privileged waterway for its contacts with the south.

Two deep sea depressions which run almost parallel, the Persian Gulf and the Red Sea (the latter extended by the Gulfs of Suez and Akaba), cut a passage from the Indian Ocean into Asia. They provide the quickest commercial routes between Asia and the West and, even taking into consideration the risks of sailing along steep and rocky coasts strewn with reefs, also the surest. But to cross the threshold is only to begin the journey, and so from the end of the Persian Gulf, which is in some measure extended by the rivers Tigris and Euphrates, the ancient caravan routes go up past Baghdad, Mosul, Aleppo and Konia towards the ports of the Levant or the Straits of Constantinople, the gateway of eastern Europe. By crossing Iran these routes also reach the shores of the Caspian and Black Seas.

A hundred years ago the Suez canal replaced the difficult land journey at the tip of the Gulf of Suez and joined the Red Sea to the Mediterranean. Today the flow of traffic between East and West has been concentrated in the canal; the great event of the last century is still of major importance in our own time.

Thus the Middle East possesses exceptionally useful seaways which greatly reduce the length of journeys to certain favoured destinations. But these short cuts do not serve every need and long land journeys have still to be taken, such as the great transcontinental routes from the Far East which converge on the Levant and recall the ancient, fabled Silk Route.

These routes, whether short or long, are far from easy. They are obstructed not only by mountains such as are common enough in Europe, but also by deserts which are peculiar to this part of the world and often more formidable.

The north in particular is mountainous. The European Alps, for all their impressive vastness, are puny in comparison with the mighty massif of the Taurus, the ranges of Armenia and Kurdestan, the Caucasus, Zagros and Elburz – that dense, complex and tortuous system where the watercourses more often carve out inaccessible gorges than negotiable valleys. Further, much of the coast of the Levant, the Red Sea and the Persian Gulf is dominated by heights steep enough to make landing impossible, such as the ranges of the Amanus, Ansariye and Lebanon, and the mountains of Sinai, the Hedjaz, Yemen and Oman.

In the less mountainous south, deserts cover vast areas and make communications equally difficult. The steppe is exhausting and discouraging because of its immensity and aridity. Sometimes volcanic rock, as in the Harra, or sand, as in the Nefud, impose additional obstacles which have to be by-passed; a whole region in eastern Arabia, the Rub al Khali, is well named the empty quarter. Yet man has largely overcome these natural barriers and thanks to him the historic role of the Middle East has been that of a highway rather than a barrier, for this part of the world has in the past held promise of fabulous riches, and still does so.

The soil of the Middle East is prodigiously fertile where there is water, and we owe to it all the fruits familiar in Europe. The rich silt of the Nile has fed heavy crops for thousands of years, and man's experience now causes cotton to grow like manna not only on the banks of the great river but in Cilicia, which not long ago was just a 'wild Egypt', and in the Jazirah – the heart of the Fertile Crescent which contours the mountains of Lebanon, Anatolia and the Zagros. Palestine, Lebanon and Syria are bedecked with orchards and soon Mesopotamia will recover her ancient fertility. Nor are these lands of Eden and Canaan famous only for the fruits of the earth; they have a magical wealth as well. For in the Middle East, or beyond it, there is always some Golden Fleece to win.

The old story of Jason has an enduring meaning. It is significant that this Greek, the first Western adventurer into the Middle East, should have braved the passage of the Straits in order to win unimaginable riches on the shores of the Caucasus. The enigmatic name of the legendary object he sought can be taken to mean either the red fleece of the mohair goat, a rare prize, or the sheepskins used by gold-washers when extracting gold from the river sands. Whichever it may have been, it conjured up a dazzling legend. The hope may have been unrealized and the treasure found disappointing, but during the course of the centuries new hopes of treasure have succeeded it. In mediaeval times it was the silks of China, the precious stones of Golconda and the spices of India that could be reached by the Middle East route; today it is oil. This quest may be succeeded by another, but in our time it is of burning importance.

There is no denying the effect of this modern Golden Fleece of Arab and Iranian oil on our own future fortunes and those of the contemporary Middle East. Its history, though short, has already been stormy. At the beginning of this century William Knox d'Arcy, an Australian geologist, guided by the evidence of some pointers from antiquity and some more precise information from a French geologist, Jacques de Morgan, made a painstaking search for oil in southern Iran and met with success at the very moment when he was about to give up in despair. Before the first World War the British Admiralty, acting through the Anglo-Iranian Oil Company, secured a controlling interest in the exploitation of the oil and a similar venture was launched in the region of Mosul.

Between the wars the vast extent of Middle Eastern oil reserves was realized; at the same time ownership became more dispersed. The British retained the monopoly in Iran, and in Iraq enjoyed the advantages of a partnership with American, Dutch and French capital in the development of the oil-fields of the Iraq Petroleum Company, whose product was piped to the Mediterranean ports of Tripoli and Haifa. In the Persian gulf, however, the British ceded their rights to the Americans, either partially as in Kuwait, or entirely as in Saudi Arabia (Aramco), where they no doubt misjudged the potentialities.

Soon after the 1939–45 war the Middle Eastern states, having realized the value of their oil reserves, began to demand a fifty-fifty share in the profits. The Americans agreed to fifty-fifty in Saudi-Arabia, but the British were slow to follow suit in Iran and were expropriated in 1951. But Iran did not succeed in selling its oil, which we replaced by stepping up production in Iraq, Kuwait and Saudi Arabia, and was obliged in 1954 to turn to an international consortium under cover of a new formula. In the meantime the oil production of the Middle East, which was lubricating the industrial rehabilitation of Europe, had been greatly expanded.

The pattern of Middle Eastern oil is becoming complicated in many ways. At present it can be rightly described as follows[1]: production, which was over 230 million tons in 1959, represents about 24% of world production; while proved reserves, which exceed 21,000 million tons, amount to as much as 80% of the supposed world resources. Of capital invested in the exploitation of these fields 60% is American, 35% Anglo-Dutch and 5% French. Owing to interlocking shareholdings the proportion of 'sterling oil' (i.e. oil for which payment can be made in sterling) is higher than these figures would indicate.

The tiny emirate of Kuwait leads the producers with 70 million tons in 1959 and provides nearly a third of the Middle Eastern total. Saudi Arabia comes second with 24%, followed by Iran (20%), Iraq (18%) and then Quatar, the neutral zone between Kuwait and Saudi Arabia, Egypt and Bahrein.

The oil is transported by pipe lines to Mediterranean ports or by tankers. The whole of the production of northern Iraq and part of the production of Saudi Arabia – i.e. a little less than a quarter of the total Middle Eastern production – are transported by pipe lines through Syrian, Jordanian and Lebanese territory to Banyas in Syria and Tripoli and Sidon in Lebanon. Most of the tankers going to Europe use the Suez canal; in 1955, to take

[1] See also Appendix II.

a 'normal' year, oil traffic, which reached nearly 67 million tons, accounted for 77% of the northbound traffic in the canal and 62% of total traffic.

These figures show how far the wealth of the Middle East depends on the smooth operation of its routes. During the crisis precipitated in the autumn of 1956 by the nationalization of the Suez canal and aggravated by the cutting of the Iraq Petroleum Company's pipe lines in Syria, the greater part of Middle Eastern oil had to go round the Cape of Good Hope in order to reach Europe, and Europe was forced by the length of this detour and by lack of tankers to buy American oil at great expense, while several Arab states, such as Saudi Arabia and above all Iraq, lost a great deal in royalties.

Chapter 2

The men who control the routes

Mention of the Suez affair is a timely reminder that material elements are not the only ones concerned. Before completing our review of the Middle East's communications and productions, we come up against the factor of the men themselves. Here again we have to note the extreme diversity of the Middle Eastern world. In race, tongue and creed the Middle East is a mosaic in which the essential features can be singled out.

The concept of race is very loose, but by adding to it the more practical criterion of language, we begin to discern a significant aspect of the human landscape of the Middle East. This region comprises three great ethno-linguistic groups: the Turks in the north, the Arabs in the south and the Iranians in the East.

There are 30 million Turks in the Republic of Turkey and the adjacent regions of the Caucasus and Iran, but they constitute only the geographic and historic extension of the Turanian masses of central Asia (Kazakhstan, Turkmenistan, etc.) who are about as numerous and who speak closely related languages.

The Arabs, who emanate from the centre of their eponymous peninsula, arabized as well as islamized various local peoples (Syrians, Aramaeans, Copts, etc.), in the course of the islamic expansion of the Middle Ages. A common language, despite small local differences of dialect, and a growing national sentiment justify the practice of calling these arabized people Arabs. On this basis there are some 50 million Arabs in Egypt, Syria, Lebanon, Jordan, Arabia, Yemen and the greater part of Iraq.

In the region which concerns us the Iranians number nearly 30 millions. Allied to the Afghans, Baluchis and Tadjiks farther East, they comprise in the Middle East not only the Persians in Iran itself but also the Kurds, who speak an Iranian language (distinct from Persian) and have a pronounced socio-national sentiment of their own. At the present time they are spread over Iran, Iraq and Turkey, with ramifications in Syria and Soviet Armenia.

We shall speak elsewhere of the Israelis, the semitic, Hebrew-speaking inhabitants of the state of Israel.

In spite of the predominance of Islam religion does not completely unify these various ethno-linguistic groups. There exist Christian groups belonging to different denominations not all of which are linked to Rome.[1] Most of them are scattered and constitute minorities of modest size but real social importance in all the states except those of the Arab peninsula. In one state, Lebanon, they comprise nearly half the population and so give the country its special character.

Jews too have always existed in the Middle East, and there are still small scattered Israelite communities in Turkey, Syria, Lebanon and Egypt, but most of the Jews of the Middle East have now joined the immigrants from central and eastern Europe to form the state of Israel, a homogeneous and increasingly important Jewish nucleus which is held together by nationalism, though not always by religion.

The Moslem majority is not homogeneous in spite of Islam's emphasis on unity and the community spirit. For a long time the Persians (but not the Kurds) and some Arabs in lower Mesopotamia and Yemen have adhered to the shiite, and the inhabitants of Muscat to the kharedjite schism, both of which originated in dissensions over the manner of choosing the Caliph and subsequently diverged yet further on theological, moral and social issues. Quite recently – during the Kemalist revolution – the Turks, who originally adopted Islam as a sort of military discipline, have laicized public life and separated church and state in defiance of Moslem tradition. Finally, agnosticism has had an impact in some places, especially in more sophisticated circles, although Islam, being by its very nature both a religious doctrine and a social and political way of life, continues effective-

[1] Cf. the Author's *Les chrétiens d'Orient*.

ly and visibly to command the loyalty of Moslems regardless of their deeper spiritual convictions.

In the course of history Islam has lent its support to various conquerors who have unified the Middle East and left fabulous memories behind – the Omayyads in Damascus, the Abbassids in Baghdad, the Fatimites, Ayubites and Mamelukes in Cairo and the Ottoman Turks in Constantinople. But although these dynasties were in accord with Islam's unitarianism to the extent that they imposed a centralized dominion over the scattered peoples of the Middle East, they also thereby prevented this part of the world from playing its proper role of intermediary and highway between East and West in that they isolated it and sealed it off. In the Middle Ages the economy of the Western world showed signs of reaction against this impediment to world trade (which was one of the sources of the crusading movement); and at the beginning of the modern age, when the Mamelukes and Mongols interrupted the direct communication between Europe and Asia, the Portuguese retaliated by making the epic journey round the Cape of Good Hope, which incidentally enabled them to take the East in the rear.

In the sixteenth century, the Ottoman empire assumed in its turn a dominion over the Middle East even more complete than its predecessors since it held Constantinople and capped the conquest of Cairo and Baghdad with the possession of Tunis, Belgrade and Budapest – and very nearly Vienna too. Gradually the Turks reopened the trade routes, although the decline of the empire after the end of the eighteenth century makes it difficult to distinguish intelligent concession from weakness in the face of European intervention. In any case Europe was able to reopen the direct route to the Indies across territories under Turkish rule or suzerainty.

In the nineteenth century the British staked out by various means a veritable Royal Road to empire on this foreign soil. By guaranteeing the integrity of the Ottoman empire they kept the Sultan under a kind of protectorship which gave them full freedom of action, while at the same time within that empire itself they set about acquiring exclusive influence over certain strategically placed tribes, such as the Shammar of northern Arabia who were in a position to dominate the shortest land route between the Mediterranean and the Persian Gulf. They studied the possibilities of modernising traditional routes, such as the Euphrates, and on the borders of the Ottoman empire they negotiated 'Advisory Treaties' with the minor potentates of the Persian Gulf who thus became their subsidiaries. Eventually these British manoeuvres were crossed by the rival imperialism of Germany which produced the Baghdad railway scheme for a line from Berlin to Baghdad by way of Belgrade, Constantinople, Aleppo and Mosul. After the 1914–18 war this line was slowly completed, but without its original imperialist trappings.

In the middle of the nineteenth century the French, though without the same political ambitions, were behind the construction of the Suez canal, which completely restored to the modern Middle East its old vocation of a highway. The initial hesitations of the British indirectly confirmed the importance of the scheme; and the khedive in Cairo, like his suzerain the Sultan in Constantinople, granted and guaranteed the concession, which was subsequently supplemented by an international convention. This new route was fully vindicated by a great increase in trade and it soon became one of the world's most important seaways.

Although conceived as an essentially peaceful enterprise, the Suez canal became in its turn involved in the conflicts of the times. At first the British secured political control by their occupation of Egypt in 1882; and even after granting independence to Egypt in 1922 and expunging the last traces of their rule in 1936 they continued to maintain garrisons in the canal zone which were only relinquished, and that unwillingly, in May 1956. For although the control of the canal ceased to be an imperial necessity after Indian independence, the canal itself remained a strategic key point and a source of political influence in the Middle East, and for these very reasons Egypt was bent on eliminating foreign control.

Prompted by such considerations the Egyptian government,

in July 1956, nationalized the concession granted to the Universal Suez Canal Company. Although the official version of the measure was the need to find money to build the Aswan dam, it was no less openly an expression of that extreme nationalist intransigence which had illegally extended the Arab blockade of Israel to traffic using the canal. The British and French reaction to the nationalization of the canal went to the length of active hostilities, which were quickly brought to an end by international pressure; but the canal, 'sabotaged' by the Egyptians, was out of commission for several months and Middle Eastern oil had to be routed round the Cape in the face of considerable difficulties. Once again the disputes of men had prevented the Middle East from fulfilling its role as a thoroughfare, to the detriment of all concerned.

After this summary historical survey some conclusions can be drawn about the basic character of this part of the world. Just as a chessboard consists of alternate black and white squares, so the Middle East juxtaposes easy passage and deceptively grim barriers; but the latter, though formidable, are not insurmountable, and in the last resort it is by men and not by nature that the Middle East has from time to time been blocked and shuttered.

A quick looked at the historic routes of the Middle East shows not only their perennial importance but also the decisive influence of local politics on the world-wide destinies of this area; either it is accessible and enriched by the flow of international commerce, or it is withdrawn and bypassed by the rest of the world. The enterprise and ingenuity of Western pioneers have, from earliest times, found ways through its natural obstacles. Jason braved the tempests of the Black Sea; Xenophon crossed the most intimidating ranges in the country of the Corduci, the Kurdistan of today; and Alexander traversed the whole region in every direction and carried the Greek genius to Asia's Buddhist lands.

Although in the thirteenth century Marco Polo's overland route to the Far East seemed an amazing and audacious new departure, in fact he was only briefly reopening the ancient Silk

Route and rediscovering the road by which Nestorian missionaries had first brought the Christian faith to Asia. For in the interval Islam had let down a curtain between Europe and Asia; radiating from Mecca along the caravan routes which had made that city of commerce and human intercourse in defiance of the surrounding deserts, it had tried to monopolize the routes which it had developed and reanimated.

Thereafter the West was forced to undertake long, though fruitful, detours. In the fifteenth century Diaz and Gama, taking the defensive offensive, rounded the Cape and arrived in the rear of the Moslem Middle East, and in the eighteenth century Admiral Orlov's Russian fleet burst through the straits of Gibraltar into the Mediterranean and unbarred the gateway of Constantinople. In the nineteenth century the efforts of the West to open up the great highways of the world and to ensure free passage of the Straits and the Suez canal were frequently frustrated by events or, more precisely, by Eastern countermoves; and then the old detours reassumed their previous importance in new forms. Thus Soviet Russia, faced with a hostile Turkey, tried in 1945 to secure a Balkan way into the Mediterranean through Albania, and British and French oil interests, faced with Arab nationalism, were forced in 1956 to revert to the discarded Cape route. In these ancient lands current events may at any moment give fresh point to the lessons of history.

Chapter 3

The forces at work

Of the dominant forces at work in the Middle East today, perhaps the first to mention is the clash between 'tradition' and 'progress'. These two rival forces struggle, fight and often compromise according to the exigencies of the moment, but in the contest between them the human elements which motivate them play a vital role and leave their mark. We should not therefore use phrases like 'modernizing trends', 'Western influence' and 'Moslem traditionalism' without attaching these concepts to the specific social groups which incarnate them severally or in combinations.

Since we must concentrate on essentials, we have to pass over a number of curious and even characteristic phenomena which are of minor importance in the overall picture, and reduce to five the operative and often unstable forces which are central to the structure and evolution of the contemporary Middle East. These five are: the desire of the Christians of the Middle East for emancipation; attempts to reform and revivify Islam; the development of Middle Eastern nationalisms (Turkish, above all Arab, and then Israeli); the rearguard action of local conservatism; and the ambitions, pressures and incursions of the outside world. The origins and structure of these forces are briefly described before showing how they affect the structure and life of the Middle East today.

To begin with, let us recall the existence and role of the Christians in the Middle East, who are so often, unfairly and shortsightedly, overlooked by Western Christendom. Although they are only small minorities, they once were and still remain a powerful agent without whom the Middle East would not have attained its present shape so rapidly or so completely.

In these lands of transit the local Christians have played the role of go-between, drawn to the West by a common faith, by their part in the West's earliest commercial ventures, by their dependence (at first total and always considerable) on the West for their education, and by their function as interpreters of the West's social and political thought and frequently as agents of its enterprise. From the middle of the nineteenth century Christian families such as the Yazigis, Bustanis, Taklas and Jumayyils laid the foundations of the renaissance of Arab culture, and later Neguib Azzuri, Shukri Ganem, Khairallah Khairallah, Edmond Rabbath, Faris al-Khuri and others pioneered the political emancipation of the Middle East.

But, as frequently happens with a small group of innovators, their very success led to their supersession and even rejection by the Moslem masses to whose awakening they contributed so greatly. Today they seem to have retreated into the background but their part is not yet played out.

Some, like Salama Musa, remain in the vanguard of social progress. Others (and here one could name a dozen or so Beirut politicians, journalists and notabilities from Henri Pharaon to Georges Naccache) tirelessly maintain the modern tradition of tolerance in an interdominational Lebanon which is the best possible intermediary between East and West. Some stoutly try to work for a sophisticated understanding with their Moslem fellow citizens, whether in the realm of thought through the magazine *Proche-Orient chrétien*, or in action (the Maronite patriarchate). Without them the Middle East would have less character, less flavour and less charm, for they are the salt and the leaven.

Virtually at the same moment as the Christians in the Middle East were awakening to this new calling, Islam was in the throes of a multifarious renaissance which has already proved infinitely fertile but is not yet completed. Faced with the decline of the Ottoman empire and almost worldwide Western colonization, the more enlightened Moslems of the Middle East saw that reform was an urgent necessity. Such were Ahmed Khan, Jamal ad-Din al-Afghani, Mohammed Abduh, Abdel-Rahman Kawakibi and Rashid Rida. They turned back to the Koran and to the teaching and practices of their great forebears, the salaf, while adopting Western ideas with a mixture of boldness and a sense of continuity.[1]

But since Islam is a way of social and political life as well as a spiritual doctrine, their activities found expression in many fields of public life. Islam exalts the idea of a Moslem community, the value of the Arab language – vehicle of the divine Revelation – and the providential prospects of a developing Middle East provided that it is saved from the domination of Western powers, and from the risks of corruption of its political and social values through contact with the West. From these concepts arise those bogys which scare the West and are called by it 'panislamism' and 'panarabism'.

The reform movement is equally capable of producing the boldest freedom of thought completely without practical effect (as with Ali Abd al-Razak) or a dogmatic and self-contained reaction which gravitates in the realm of politics towards totalitarianism and the mediaeval Koranic state (as with the Moslem Brotherhood). In a wider sense the reform movement has permanently enhanced the socio-religious values of Islam in the Middle East by preparing the ground for their stimulating conjunction with Arab nationalism.

Nationalism is an emanation of the West and particularly of the French Revolution. Spreading to the East, it first contributed to the disintegration of the Ottoman empire by encouraging the formation of national states by Christian peoples such as the Greeks, Serbs and Bulgarians in the Balkans; but as soon as it reached the Moslem world it joined forces with and drew sustenance from Islam's religious feelings and Islam's claim to regulate secular as well as spiritual life. It developed, however, in very different ways among different peoples.

In Turkey, following the boost given to Turkish pride by

[1] On the reform movement see the author's *L'islam et les musulmans d'aujourd'hui*, pp. 233 ff.

panislamic ideas, the dominant influence was the nationalism organized by Mustafa Kemal within the machinery of a modern state divorced by law from the Moslem way of life. In the case of the Arabs, there was a dual conflict. On the one hand there was conflict between modernizing and traditional forces and the outcome was determined by time and place – governments inclined to laicization, as in the Republic of Syria; nations more or less devoted to Islam as a state religion, as in Egypt and Iraq; or mediaeval kingdoms as in Saudi Arabia and Yemen. On the other, there was a second conflict between this tendency to diverge and an underlying belief in a common Arab destiny and a common Arab future. This belief took the form of a legend of unity, the effectiveness of which depended on the extent to which it became a source of rival ambitions, or found a single champion like Nasser whose prestige reached far beyond the confines of one country and inspired the Arabs with a likely belief in their own solidarity. This Arab nationalism – or these Arab nationalisms – was further provoked and unified by the growth of the rival and, in a sense, imported nationalism of Zionism.

However skilfully the reform movement was represented as a return to the past, the injection of these new ideas into an ancient society could not fail to provoke strong reactions, the more so since Western influence, discredited in the political field, tended to fan the flames of social revolution. The conservatism of the traditional Middle East has survived and emerges on numerous occasions in varying and sometimes competing forms.

Among the Christians tradition has fought against innovation and has continued to advocate, more or less openly, attachment to the less sordid aspects of the West's time-honoured protective role. Among the Moslems conservatism has replied to reformism with the literalism and archaism of the Moslem Brotherhood, for whom 'renewal' is something purely formal, and justifies the mediaevalism of Saudi Arabia and Yemen, which claim to have discovered and to be following the Islamic way of life complete and unadulterated.

Nationalism often comes to terms with the rich and powerful, who use it for their own ends. Under the traditionalist aegis of a dynasty like the Hashemites in Iraq and Jordan 'governments of pashas' could protect the interests of 'feudal lords' and the upper middle class. Further, the flow of wealth from oilfields enables the sovereign to indulge, according to taste, in benevolent despotism, in a twentieth century version of the Thousand and One Nights, or in political corruption which substitutes false for genuine ideals.

Both progressive and reactionary movements give ample opportunities for the outside world to interfere. Though the age of colonialism be dead and open protectorates (outside certain tribal enclaves) no longer practicable, dominion can take subtler forms in the hope that they will be more lasting.

For example, there was the independence hurriedly granted to Iraq in 1930–32 but unobtrusively laced with unequal clauses. There was the influence, for all practical purposes an exclusive if indirect influence, exercised in southern Iran through the oil company. And there is the technical, financial and economic aid offered by both the U.S.S.R. and the U.S.A. with a variety of unspoken motives. There is propaganda in all its forms, setting the 'free world' with its moral precepts and economic advantages against the 'popular democracies' proffering infallible methods for breaking imperialist yokes and practical recipes for progress in under-developed areas.

The Middle East is a target for all these manoeuvres and is only partly deceived. It tries in its turn to bamboozle its would-be seducers, but the disparity in material resources often places it at a disadvantage.

These then are the forces which must now be surveyed in the hard light of history since the end of the first World War. At each stage of the story, there must be an attempt to isolate the principal factor in the Middle East's destiny in the hope of singling out *the* Eastern Question which may be different at different times but is always in its own time unique and preponderant, and secretly controls the seething confusion of trends and facts.

PART III

THE PERIOD OF ARAB NATIONALISM (1919–36)

CHAPTER 1

The decline of the Ottoman Empire

THE POLITICAL MAP of the Middle East today dates from the early nineteen-twenties. In spite of many changes of frontier and even of names of states nothing basic has altered in thirty years. The political map of 1960 recalls in broad outline that of 1930, but both are strikingly different from the map of 1914. It was the first World War that brought today's Middle East into being, or more precisely it was the downfall of the Ottoman empire that permitted the balkanization of western Asia which had previously been united under Turkish rule.

We must briefly recall what the Ottoman empire was – not for any pedantic historical reason but because so ancient and vast a structure does not crumble without leaving traces behind.

The Ottoman empire once filled Europe with fear and horror by means of its military and naval power, the extent of its conquests and the harsh rule which it exercised right up to the gates of Vienna. France was the first to see that the Turks could be made to play a role in European balance-of-power politics and made them a back-door ally in the sixteenth century. In the eighteenth century Britain too subscribed to this idea and once the Turks had been displaced from the centre of Europe by the liberation of Austria and Hungary, the Ottoman empire became a serviceable check to Russian ambitions which were beginning to threaten the eastern Mediterranean, Constantinople and the land approaches to the British empire in India. The Ottoman empire filled a vacuum which might have become an abyss.

Hence arose the classic Eastern Question of how to keep this crumbling empire neither too feeble nor too active, how to keep the 'sick man' alive without actually curing him. To state the problem is easy enough but its solution was rendered difficult by a number of supervening factors of disconcerting complexity. In short, the peoples – mainly Christian – long subjugated by the Ottoman empire wished to live, and live free.

For several centuries the French monarchy had found a solution which was acceptable to its Turkish allies the Sultans, and thanks to French protection the Christian communities of the Middle East became securer in the enjoyment of greater rights – religious liberty, human dignity and even equal civil rights, but not as yet political freedom. Then Revolutionary France launched a new ideal – the emancipation of nationalities – which was further defined in the course of the nineteenth century, and which was held to apply to the subject peoples in the Ottoman empire. In 1828 France and Britain helped Greece to free itself.

But to apply this principle too far and too fast would have meant the complete collapse of the Ottoman empire. The Russians proposed to force the sultan to choose, in Gortschakoff's gruesome play on words, between 'autonomy and anatomy' unless the Christians under the Tsar's protection were completely emancipated – a radical dissection very much in the Russian interest. Moreover, it soon became apparent that the Ottoman Christians were not the only peoples affected. Almost immediately after the Greek revolt Egypt contrived to obtain a degree of autonomy not far short of independence, and elsewhere in the empire new leaders of countries which were either predominantly Moslem (such as the Arabs) or completely Moslem (as the Turks themselves) were formulating claims against the Sublime Porte in liberal and nationalist terms.

At the opening of the twentieth century the Ottoman empire seemed doomed to shrink and to disappear at some future date. Faced with this prospect the policies of the Powers diverged, and certain characteristics which were to persist to our own time became observable.

Germany alone among the European Powers wanted to keep the Ottoman empire intact, but this policy masked an ambition to make the whole empire a German fief. Kaiser William advertised his great respect for the Sultan and Caliph of Islam and professed himself his champion, but under cover he organized economic penetration which was massive in scale and exclusive in intention; the grand scheme for a Baghdad railway was at once the symbol and the instrument of his policy. Behind Germany its second string, Austria-Hungary, reserved for itself dominion over the small liberated Balkan states and in this way the two Powers together sought to erect a solid barrier against Russian ambitions from the Danube to the Caucasus.

The Tsars meanwhile, following Catherine the Great's 'Greek project', were stubbornly pursuing the grand design of effacing Turkish dominion and replacing it by a host of small dependent states. From the middle of the nineteenth century the other Powers effectively thwarted this plan and from time to time supported the sultan for this purpose; in 1878, for example, the Russian armies were halted at the very gates of Constantinople. But Russian penetration went on indirectly and worked upon the independent Christian states in the Balkans – Slav (Serbia, Bulgaria) or at any rate Orthodox (Greece) – and upon the still subject Christians, especially the Armenians, who were pushed into desperate risings fated to be drowned in blood, as in 1895.

This impatience of the subject races prevented the British from persevering in their original policy of exercising a discreet protectorate over a paralysed empire such as Stratford Canning could still exercise in mid-century over Abdul Mejid. Britain had increasingly to take emergent nationalities into its calculations but it also took a decision of great practical wisdom. Among the Christians Britain was content to counterbalance Russian and French influences but among the Moslem, the Druzes and particularly the Arabs, it sought special contacts and began to try to create vassal states like Egypt, which was occupied in 1882 and completely detached and formally converted into a protectorate on the outbreak of war in 1914.

France persisted in its age-old policy, admirable in itself, of protecting the rights of the Christians in the Levant. France could claim never to have altered its policy from the time of St. Louis to the days of Louis XIV, the Convention and the emissaries of the Third Republic, Constant and Bompard; and when Napoleon III gallantly proclaimed that his solicitudes for the troubles of Christians would be extended to Moslem grievances as well, he was only confirming established French practice. Schools and hospitals were built by the French for all and so France more than any other Power nurtured liberal and national movements at their very foundations. But since the French simply reckoned that the empire would become more tolerant as it became weaker, they failed to perceive that their own traditional attitude might cease to have any meaning for the successor states, if these were really free. Generous and disinterested though it was, French policy in the Middle East was destined to become less and less effective and to be outdated by the very advances which it encouraged.

For better or worse the Ottoman empire lived on in the midst of these policies, propped up by their contradictions. Sometimes, yielding to fate, it relinquished sovereignty totally (Libya, Rhodes) or partially (Cyprus, Egypt) or conceded local autonomy (Mount Lebanon, Mecca and the Holy Places of Islam); at other times it tried to retain or recover authority by force of arms (Yemen). In its progressive decline it acquired none the less a touch of modernization from its European contacts. Europe, while constricting the empire in the loose meshes of the Ottoman debt, also equipped it with ports, mines and railways. The best of its subjects sensed the possibility of a national renascence through the use of the country's natural resources. Sailors released from naval service were shown pieces of coal by their officers and urged to look for similar objects in the ground round their villages, and this pre-industrial movement led to the discovery of the coal seams of Zonguldak. For this exhausted empire retained a sort of rustic efficiency which it derived from the long established exercise of an authority which was confident, unquestioned and at the same time niggardly. In the Anatolian provinces officials were hard and mistrustful in their dealings with the Christians whom they suspected of owing allegiance to foreigners, but in the Arab provinces they were milder. One of them, a man who became an important Arab politician, told the author how at the beginning of his career he held a civilian post on the borders of the Hedjaz, where he administered a small fund for the benefit of Syrian recruits who were sent to Yemen on military service – too thankless a task to be performed by the Turks themselves. Through negligence or for economic reasons these young Syrians were not released when their time was up; but if they got tired of waiting and decided to make their own way home, they were given a little help along the road by the officials who ought to have been arresting them as deserters.

Such was the Ottoman empire at the end, a listless despot, a subtle but exhausted tyrant over an inorganic Middle East. It seemed to be virtually irreplaceable but, so the realistic British told themselves, since it must die soon in spite of every care, better make provision against the day. They alone thought of a substitute in good time: to create an Arab empire which would take the place of the Ottoman one and be similarly protected.

CHAPTER 2

The first sparks of Arab nationalism

FASCINATED BY THE British system of Parliamentary government and by the French theory of nationalism, Turkish and Arab progressives found inspiration and support in western Europe. The first Young Turk newspaper appeared in 1868 in London, but it was in Paris that the Committee of Union and Progress was founded in 1894 and shortly afterwards the Arab Patriotic League and the Ottoman Arab Fraternity. Neguib Assuri's *Réveil de la nation arabe* was published in Paris in 1905 and the first Arab National Congress met there in 1913. Beirut and Damascus, the two cities of the Levant most open to European influence, were the homes of Arab Committees which, while openly preaching awakening and decentralization and reform, were secretly fostering independence. And finally the modern Arab press was launched by Lebanese Christians in Cairo thanks to an open mind about Western ways on the part of the khedival dynasty (the Sultan's nominal and restless vassals), to the advantages of reform of the administration effected by the British, and to the general progress inspired by the presence of foreign communities.

The Young Turks seized power in Constantinople in 1908 and for a moment it seemed as if the parliament which they re-established and which included some, if too few, Arab members might breathe new life into Ottoman organs. But this was not to be; there emerged only a new and no more efficient depotism. External defeats – by Italy in 1912 and by the Balkan coalition in 1913 – encouraged on the contrary a new wave of mistrustful xenophobia and islamic bids for fresh concessions.

The Ottoman empire made its last and fatal mistake when it

joined the German side in the war on October 30th, 1914. The Germans dominated its economy, had just overhauled its army and never stopped flattering the panislamic proclivities of its rulers. They persuaded the sultan-caliph to proclaim on November 23rd a holy war against 'Russia, France, England and their allies, the mortal enemies of Islam'. This appeal had no effect on the Moslem units from North Africa, India and Turkestan which were serving with the allied armies, nor did it prevent a few months later the Arabian revolt which was fomented by the sherif of Mecca with British help.

The British had been following the national awakening of the Arab peoples for a long time and had been encouraging it when they could. Unlike Paris and the French consulate in Beirut they did not merely meet intellectuals and applaud their appeals; they went further. They made contacts with traditional notables, officers of Arab origin, tribal chiefs and religious leaders and they took more interest in the semi-desert, semi-liberated parts of Arabia than in the turbulent cities of the Levant. They saw in these steppes an area easier to control, flanked as it was by the canal and Egypt and by the route to India; and prompted by such considerations they had been making the most varied contacts since before the war.

It was therefore no surprise that on the outbreak of hostilities the British should receive in Cairo emissaries from the sherif Hussein of Mecca. This eminent descendant of the Prophet held the holy places of Islam subject to the remote suzerainty of the sultan-caliph and in his name. Eager to throw off this allegiance the sherif underlined the uncanonical character of the holy war proclaimed at Constantinople and, over and above his personal predisposition to rebellion, made the most of the resolutions in favour of action which had been passed in Damascus in his sons' presence by the secret committees and particularly by *al Ahd*, the organ of the Arab officers in the Ottoman army.

There ensued an exchange of letters between the British High Commissioner in Egypt, Sir Henry MacMahon, and the sherif Hussein, which lasted from July 14th, 1915, to January 30th,

1916. By this correspondence, which was never put in the form of a definite agreement signed by both sides, the British promised to cede complete independence to the Arab countries with the sole exceptions of the crown colony of Aden, lower Mesopotamia, where Britain reserved certain rights, and a part of the Levant coast where French influences were paramount.

This last reservation was to have considerable historical importance, since it was later invoked by the British to justify their zionist policy in Palestine. Twenty years later Sir Henry MacMahon himself confirmed that 'in giving this promise to King Hussein it was not his intention to include Palestine in the area in which Arab independence had been promised'. But the text of the controversial document, officially published by the British only at this late date, was in any case somewhat ambiguous : 'The two districts of Mersina and Alexandretta and portions of Syria lying to the west of the districts of Damascus, Homs, Hama and Aleppo cannot be said to be purely Arab and should be excluded from the limits demanded. . . . As for those regions lying within those frontiers wherein Great Britain is free to act without detriment to the interests of her ally France . . . Great Britain is prepared to recognize and support the independence of the Arabs.' [1]

But this difficulty was not to be raised until, after the war, the Jewish National Home was installed in Palestine. For the time being the British undertakings seemed adequate and the revolt was launched. On June 10th, 1916, the sherif made a declaration of Arab independence to the commander of the Turkish garrison at Mecca who refused to surrender, retaliated and even shelled the Kaaba. In a long proclamation on June 27th, Hussein justified his rebellion by accusing the sultan-caliph of failing in his observation of islamic law and in his secular duties, and by making a point of the execution of Syrian conspirators who had belonged to secret Arab societies. On November 6th he had himself proclaimed King of the Arabs, a title to which the British

[1] Cmd 5957, pp. 7–9.

would have preferred the more modest one of King of the Hedjaz.

A British archaeologist whom this venture was to render famous, Colonel T. E. Lawrence, was entrusted with the mission of organizing the revolt and leading the Arabs into battle. Their exploits on the flanks of Allenby's army had little military significance but Lawrence achieved a tremendous political feat, for he laid the foundations of the destiny of Arab nationalism.

Lawrence's deeds and writings long fascinated the West, which saw him as a kind of universal and mysterious genius. Since his detractors have attacked the legend of the scholar-soldier, many people have come to think of him as no more than an impostor, but to do so is to ignore the fact that his part in the desert revolt formed the basis of a political structure which still to some extent persists in the Middle East today and which owed much to the judgment of men displayed by the author of the *Seven Pillars of Wisdom*.

Among the sons of the sherif Hussein who were directly associated with him and whom he was able to test in the Arab microcosm of the tribes in revolt – whether in the subtleties of council or the emergencies of action – Lawrence picked out Abdullah, the subtle man of letters, shrewd and resourceful, for complex but yet secondary tasks, while choosing his younger brother Feisal for the leading role. In the younger emir, whom his father had shrewdly sent to perfect his insight and his political education among tribesmen, Lawrence discerned not only an adequate adaptability to Western ideas and a high capacity for authority and organization, but also a gift for stirring Arab hearts – in fact, the all-important ability to influence this world of the future.

So Lawrence backed Feisal and, prompted perhaps by that ambiguous temperament to which his complicated prose bears witness, he deliberately subordinated himself. He took a second place, curbed every desire for direct action or strict control and sacrificed his *amour-propre* to such an extent that he sometimes seemed to put his dream for the Arabs over and above the interests and dignity of his own country. In fact, however, he won for Britain the only positions, peripheral and unobtrusive, which could be serviceable and lasting in the new Middle East and (hence our insistence on this man and his doings) he originated the British policy, which was to last for a quarter of a century, of indirect control through the medium of Arab nationalism.

Lawrence never had any illusions about the virtues and qualities of the Arabs, in particular about their constructive and organizing capacities; he has himself written in the plainest terms of the hours of weariness and disgust which they cost him. What a degree of disillusionment there is in the following story, for example. A camel driver urged by Lawrence to attend to the sores of his camel broke into a long lamentation on the miseries of the Arabs under the Turkish yoke and enthusiastically hailed the coming Arab empire and the grand projects it would undertake, including a veterinary college which would wipe out animal diseases by the most modern means – and then let his poor beast die for want of the simplest care. Lawrence smiled bitterly but he did not let this little incident, on top of many others, induce him to relinquish his Arab schemes.

When Lawrence's little Anglo-Arab force appeared before the gates of Damascus on September 30th, 1918, its leader could hardly have been under any illusions about its real contribution to the military victory which had in fact been won by Allenby over the Turkish army in Palestine, nor could he conceal from himself the fact that the success of his bold expedition owed much more to himself than to the sherifian prince. But he effaced himself in order that the people might see their liberation as an Arab achievement, and he left Feisal and his people to make their entry into the recovered city of Damascus without him. This gesture symbolized and hallowed Britain's Arab policy which was to dominate the Middle East for fifteen years.

From then on the new national movement had a flag which combined the Arab colours: the green of the Prophet and the first caliphs, the white of the Omayyads, the black of the Abbasids and the red of the Hashemites. By using these colours in different combinations the various Arab states were thereafter to have standards of their own while also affirming their unity. To this ambivalence, which was not discernible at that time, there was added at the outset a second and more serious one. This Arab flag was devised by a British diplomat and historian of the East, Sir Mark Sykes, who was negotiating a partition of Arab lands among Britain and its allies at the same time as he was creating a symbol of Arab unity.

Right from the start British policy lacked the absoluteness of Hussein's and Feisal's dreams – and perhaps of Lawrence's too, since Lawrence did not have the field to himself. As the policy came to be applied, it had to take account of this contingency or that, give heed to the interests of allies and even of adversaries, and allow the play of other forces. Hence a chain of political actions and manœuvres which annoyed everybody in greater or less degree; Britain's Western partners and its non-Arab Eastern associates often believed themselves let down or even betrayed, and the Arabs themselves saw their (perhaps excessive) hopes disappointed, became mistrustful of Britain's goodwill and were even led on occasion to turn towards Britain's enemies. The British were accused of double-dealing from all sides, the more so because they were envied for their skill.

But the British, who were quite capable of realistic deviations from the absolute ideals of their Arab friends, nevertheless kept any concessions or compromises subordinate to the central conception of their Arab policy. Sometimes they almost cynically sacrificed everything to this conception. And Britain's role in the Middle East in this period was so considerable that it is proper to consider this phase of Middle Eastern history – the phase of Arab national self-assertion – from the standpoint of British policy.

But first certain arrangements should come under review, arrangements apart from and even inimical to the Arab movement, to which London gave its consent. The first and most serious coincided with the Hussein–MacMahon exchanges and consisted of a scheme to partition the Arab world and put it under the protection of outside Powers. This scheme was first formulated in secret agreements between the allies in 1915–17: the Anglo-Franco-Russian agreement of March 4th, 1915, and tripartite convention of February 19th, 1916; the Sykes-Picot agreement of May 16th, 1916, between Britain and France; and the agreement of St.-Jean-de-Maurienne with Italy on August 21st, 1917.

There is no point in going into the concessions made to the Russians in Anatolia since they were nullified by later events, but it is necessary to give a brief account of the Franco-British arrangement which was primarily concerned with the Arab parts of the Middle East. In the Sykes-Picot agreement these areas were to receive neither the near-unity nor the complete independence envisaged in the Hussein-McMahon correspondence. They were partitioned into spheres of influence and administered areas: (1) zones christened A (French influence) consisting of the vilayets of Damascus, Aleppo and Mosul; and B (British influence) consisting of the territories between Palestine and southern Mesopotamia where there was to be established 'an independent Arab State or a confederation of Arab States' which would give the interested Powers 'priority of right of enterprise and local loans' and the exclusive right to supply 'advisers and foreign functionaries'; and (2) a 'blue' zone (French administration) consisting of Cilicia, southern Anatolia, the Syria coast and Lebanon; a 'red' zone (British administration) consisting of southern Mesopotamia with the addition of the British enclave of Haifa and Acre; and finally a 'brown' zone (international administration) consisting of Palestine and the holy places. The management of these coloured zones was to take the form of direct or indirect rule or of supervision by agreement with the Arab state or confederation.[1]

These arrangements, although imprecise and never applied in this form, were of cardinal importance. They contained the germ of the division of the Arab countries into British and French mandates, once they had been freed from Turkish rule.

[1] See map opposite.

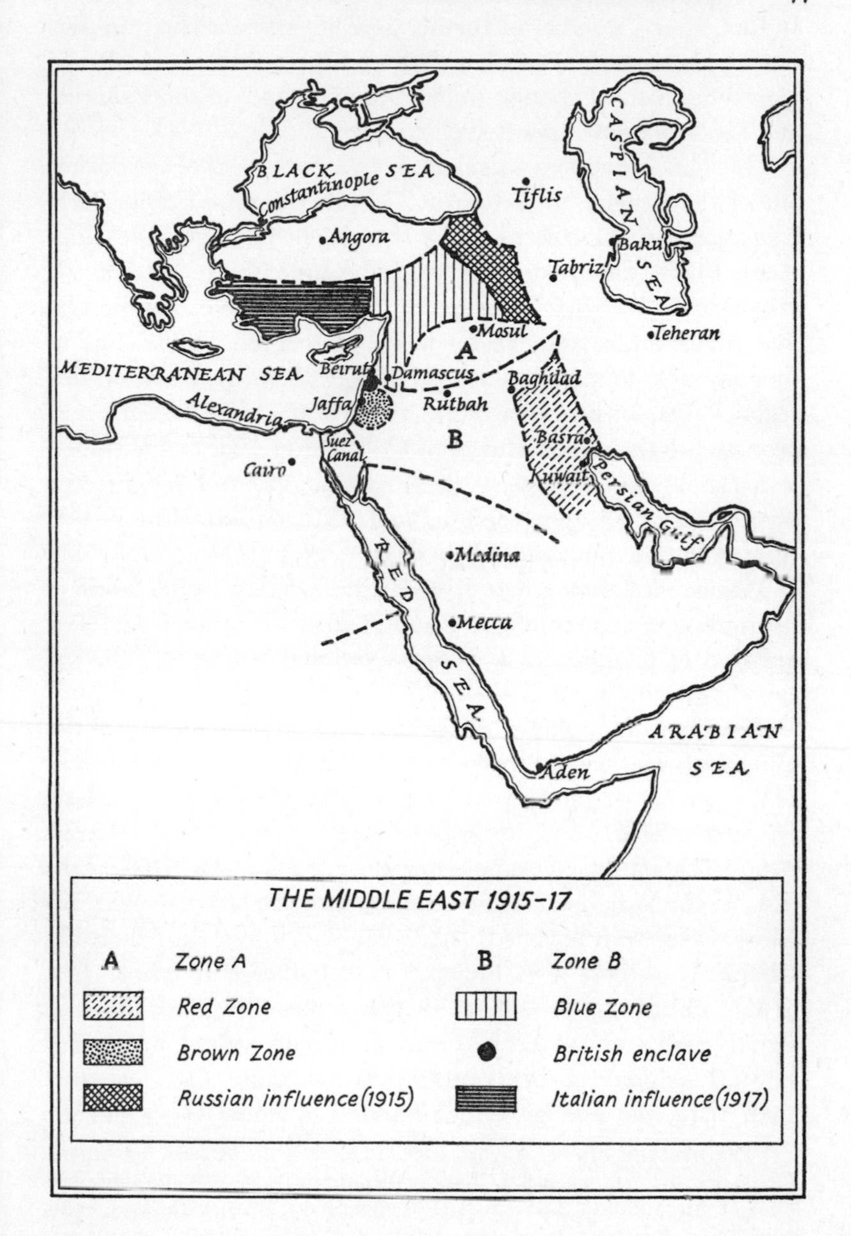
BLACK SEA
Constantinople
Angora
Tiflis
CASPIAN SEA
Baku
Tabriz
Teheran
Mosul
A
MEDITERRANEAN SEA
Beirut
Damascus
Baghdad
Jaffa
Rutbah
Alexandria
B
Basra
Suez Canal
Cairo
Kuwait
Persian Gulf
Medina
RED SEA
Mecca
ARABIAN SEA
Aden
THE MIDDLE EAST 1915-17
A Zone A
B Zone B
Red Zone
Blue Zone
Brown Zone
British enclave
Russian influence (1915)
Italian influence (1917)

In fact, after a number of further agreements restricting, in particular, the zone of French influence,[1] the treaty of San Remo placed Syria and Lebanon under French mandate and Palestine and Mesopotamia under British mandate.

The mandate system was laid down in article 22 of the covenant of the League of Nations: 'Certain communities formerly belonging to the Turkish Empire had reached a stage of development where their existence as independent nations can be provisionally recognized subject to the rendering of administrative advice and assistance by a Mandatory until such time as they are able to stand alone.' Although liberal in intention this régime was a far cry from the complete 'independence' promised to the sheriff Hussein. Arab nationalism entered upon a tenacious revolt against these restrictions and against the divisions imposed upon the liberated Arab regions. How Britain reacted in this dilemma will be seen.

Meanwhile London had opened a new breach in the fabric of its Arab dreams, though promoting these in other ways. The question of establishing a Jewish National Home in Palestine raised its head.

The zionist movement, whose aim since the second half of the nineteenth century had been the rehabilitation and resettlement of the persecuted Jewish people, adopted at the Congress of Basle on August 24th, 1897, the express aim to create 'for the Jewish people a home in Palestine secured by public law'. During the first World War the Zionists entered into negotiations with Sir Mark Sykes with a view to realizing this object, on which Dr. Chaim Weizmann was insisting in no uncertain terms. This Jewish chemist, who was of British nationality, had rendered signal service to the British war effort and sought no reward beyond the grant of this boon to his community. On November 2nd, 1917, the Foreign Office handed to Lord Rothschild the

[1] The treaty of Sèvres, August 10th, 1920, and the Ankara agreement, October 20th, 1921, extending Turkey's southern frontier to a point on the Gulf of Alexandretta; the San Remo agreements, April 18th–25th, 1920, confirming the transfer of the Mosul area and Palestine to British influence.

Balfour Declaration, whereby the British government declared that they 'view with favour the establishment in Palestine of a National Home for the Jewish people and will use their best endeavours to facilitate the achievement of this object.'

From that day the Arabs observed the anniversary of the Balfour Declaration as a day of national mourning. The British did their best, though with little permanent result, to set bounds to the political effects of this undertaking; but however strictly it was interpreted, it struck the Arabs as an unpardonable derogation from the Arab unity which Sir Henry MacMahon had dangled before the eyes of the sherif Hussein.

Britain imposed a third limitation on its contribution to the emanicipation of the Arabs when it adopted a restrictive policy in Egypt in spite of that country's eagerness for independence.

At this period Egypt was still on the periphery of the Arab movement. It was not included in the demand presented on January 29th, 1919, by the emir Feisal to the Peace Conference that the arabic speaking peoples of Asia should be recognized as independent sovereign peoples. Similarly there was no mention of the word 'Arab' in the memorandum in which Saad Zaghlul Pasha, the leader of the Wafd delegation, presented 'Egypt's national claims'. This document represented the Egyptian people as a distinct ethnic block which assimilates foreign elements so that they lose their special characteristics; and it even concluded that when Europe decided that the Hedjaz, only yesterday a Turkish province, had a right to independence, it could not fail to treat Egypt, infinitely more developed and already autonomous, on at least an equal footing. Far from championing the Arab movement, Egypt scented in it a dangerous rival.

In fact Egypt, viceregal vassal of the Ottoman empire, occupied by the British in 1882 and turned into a protectorate on December 18th, 1914, had long cherished its own national movement. The key figures of this Egyptian nationalism were its founder Mustafa Kemal; next, Saad Zaghlul, the Wafd leader who secured from the British on February 28th, 1922, a declaration recognizing 'Egypt to be an independent sovereign state' but reserving to the British government certain important functions, particularly in matters of imperial communications and defence; and finally Mustafa Nahas, the lieutenant and eventual successor of Zaghlul who after a fierce struggle obtained the treaty of August 26th, 1936, which effected the complete liberation of the country with the exception of the British right to station forces in the Canal Zone and to use that territory in time of war.

The whole of this development of the relations between Cairo and London took place outside the ambit of the Arab movement. Many Egyptian patriots prided themselves on being 'pharaonic' and thought of themselves as Arabs only by tongue. But this linguistic link, combined with the religious one, promoted political solidarity and it soon became decisive. Particularly after 1930 Egyptian nationalist opinion became more attuned to that of the Arabs of Asia, urging resistance to imperialism and exalting Moslem values but also ambitious to see Cairo supreme. The religious importance of the Egyptian capital, the traditional influences of the university of al Azhar, the up-to-date glamour of reformism, the strength and quality of the national leadership, the material resources of the country – all these things told in favour of Egypt which proceeded to embrace the cause of Arab solidarity with the expectation of winning the leading place, provided only that it could outstrip its dangerous rival, Iraq.

Chapter 3

Britain and Iraq

Whereas British policy in Egypt was severely restrictive up to the war of 1939, in Iraq it was go-ahead. Britain decided – not without careful consideration of its own interests – to make the fullest use of Arab nationalism in association with a trusted ally, and deliberately and definitely selected the new Mesopotamian state to be the champion of the Arab movement. Meeting in Cairo in March 1921 Winston Churchill, Gertrude Bell, Lawrence and several other experts laid down the new lines of British policy in the Middle East and how to carry it out. An invisible air control exercised by the Royal Air Force from well guarded bases set at a distance from the main towns was to replace the irksome military occupation, and an unobtrusive tutelage, ostensibly based on honourable contractual relationships but subtly unequal in practice, was to remove the need for irksome political domination.

On August 23rd, 1921, Britain placed Feisal, who had been driven out of Damascus after quarrelling with the French, on the throne of Baghdad and set beside him one of Lawrence's tried companions, Nuri al-Said Pasha, who was destined to become the perfect interpreter of an ambitious Anglo-Arab policy. But the beginnings of the new Hashemite kingdom were not easy. The Shiite and Kurdish minorities, who together outnumbered the Sunnis, resorted to revolt or agitation, while in the capital impatient nationalists demanded independence without conditions or delay.

In the face of these difficulties the British adroitly adapted their policy; they retained such prerogatives and functions as they deemed indispensable, but exercised these as little as possible, in accordance with the decisions taken at Cairo. London's protective authority over Baghdad took the form not of tight-lipped exercise of an imposed mandate, but the execution of a negotiated treaty which was signed on October 10th, 1922. Local extremists were certainly not unaware that the agreement was a very unequal one, but to the outside world Iraq had more national glamour than any other Arab state and the principle of its rapid advance to complete independence was thenceforward clearly established.

During the short period at their disposal for helping modern Iraq to take shape, the British did their best to avoid aggravating the impatience of the nationalists by harping on the tricky problems of internal balance and administration which arose out of the existence of minorities, or on the need for harmonious economic development and social progress in order to alleviate the flagrant inequalities of wealth and living standards. Ill-timed enthusiasm in these directions would have alienated the moderate nationalists of the rich Sunni middle class, whose pursuit of influence and office led them into alliance with the Crown and the representatives of the British protecting power; it would also have given extra weapons to the extremists whose reactions sometimes ended in tragedy. The suicide of one Prime Minister, Abdul Muhsin al-Saadun, who was driven to despair by the calculated procrastination and cleverly contrived restrictions of the British High Commission, was an embarrassing warning.

But at this price Iraq, discreetly advanced and sustained by Britain and endowed with the prestige of ripening independence, played the role of pioneer of the Arab movement, a nebulous role admittedly devoid of legal basis or diplomatic substance but rich in sentimental appeal. Thenceforward the militants of the Arab nationalist ideal turned to Iraq from every quarter. Fortified by this development and anxious to give it greater impetus the British granted Iraq complete independence by the treaty of June 30th, 1930, although in modernization and efficiency the country lagged behind Lebanon, Syria and Egypt. Neither the well-founded protests of anxious minorities nor the somewhat faint objections of the Mandates Commission availed to prevent the ratification of the treaty or the entry of Iraq into the League of Nations, and these events were unfortunately soon followed by a hideous massacre of Assyrians in the Mosul district (August 11th, 1930).

Thus Iraq and its British protectors bought this ascendancy in the heady politics of the Arab world at a heavy price in concessions (to which we shall return), but for many years the government in Baghdad, and indirectly its Western ally, were the hallowed leaders of the Arab movement. From the latter part of 1930 Nuri began to exploit his success by launching the idea of an Arab alliance which would include Transjordan, Nedj and the Hedjaz as well as Iraq and eventually all the remaining Arab countries too. Failing this and in the meanwhile Baghdad would be satisfied to construct a network of bilateral agreements within the ambit of Anglo-Arab policy.

But Ibn Saud, the sovereign of Nejd, had turned King Hussein out of Mecca and had thus forced him, on October 13th, 1924, to abandon the title of caliph which he had lately assumed. Next he expelled King Ali from Jedda and annexed the Hedjaz on January 8th, 1926; in 1932 he took the title of King of Saudi Arabia. In a different way this enemy of the Hashemites put himself forward as a rival champion of panarab brotherhood, as was demonstrated in 1931 when in the course of a contest with the Imam of Yemen about Jebel Aruh he renounced his claims and conceded the disputed territory to his rival on the grounds that 'it was leaving the possession of one Arab for the possession of another'. When none the less war broke out three years later, Ibn Saud imposed on the defeated Imam the 'treaty of islamic friendship and Arab brotherhood' of May 19th, 1934, which envisaged 'perpetual islamic Arab fraternity' between them and even laid down the principle that 'the two nations were but one'. Although this was no more than a manœuvre by an intelligent ruler accentuating his magnificent generosity for propaganda purposes, gestures of this kind nurtured passions which went further than heads of state foresaw or welcomed.

The influence of the Iraqi brand of panarabism was especially effective in countries subject to foreign protection and occupation. Egypt, it is true, was immersed in its own struggle and remained isolated and mistrustful until it set up as a rival, but Syria contained many nationalists who were loyal to Feisal, regarded a return of the Hashemites as the best way of getting rid of the French mandate and saw the future in terms of a union with Iraq.

The example of the Baghdad government which had been thus tactfully installed by the British encouraged the growth of the Arab movement in every way; at some points it elicited other and rival foci of Arab unity as in Saudi Arabia and later Egypt; at others, it stimulated opposition to purely local loyalties, and to the imperialist manœuvres in the Levant states where, for instance, it promoted the Hashemite vision of a Greater Syria.

At the same time the British, so far as in them lay, deliberately sacrificed other aspects of development which could have been just as fruitful and would in any case have promoted genuine human values. By giving a start to the Iraqi incarnation of panarab nationalism the British in effect thwarted any reproductions of the Turkish renascence, sacrificed national minorities such as the Kurds and the Assyrians, undermined French policy in Syria and Lebanon, and tried to check the Zionism which they had themselves introduced into Palestine – without succeeding, on this last issue, in curbing an Arab movement which they were encouraging elsewhere.

In spite of its long years of association with the British the Ottoman empire had disappointed them by succumbing to German blandishments at the beginning of the twentieth century and the attempted reforms of the Young Turks did nothing to alter this Germanophil orientation. Consequently Britain, banking thenceforward on the Arabs to safeguard its Middle Eastern interests, completely abandoned the policy of preserving the integrity of Turkey; this it did from the time of the agreements of 1915 and more specifically with the armistice of Mudros of October 30th, 1918, and the treaty of Sèvres of August 10th, 1920. Subject to certain allied spheres of influence, Britain encouraged the rise of the subject races in what had been the Ottoman empire.

This British hostility to the fallen Turkish régime was not abated by the national and social revolution inaugurated by Mustafa Kemal in 1920 in eastern Anatolia. On the contrary, London encouraged the Greek expedition which, starting from the historic sites of Ionia, tried to re-create a Magna Grecia right round the Aegean and put the new Turkey in mortal peril before being finally swept back into the sea at Smyrna (Izmir) in September 1922.

Mustafa Kemal did not meet with the same opposition from the French; after bitter fighting in Cilicia and southern Anatolia they resigned themselves to ceding to the new Turkey the northern fringe of their allotted sphere of influence in the Levant. They entered into friendly negotiations with the Turks without however succeeding in acquiring any special advantages for themselves. They were moreover in a false position with regard to Ankara. For all their conciliatory intentions they had to defend the interests of their Syrian protégés (an obligation not always effectively discharged); they ended by agreeing in 1939 to the return of the sanjak of Alexandretta to Turkey, in contrast to the British who in 1925 secured possession of the vilayet of Mosul for Iraq.

In the first stages of his revolutionary movement Mustafa Kemal found wholehearted and effective support in the U.S.S.R. alone; he saw in the Soviets a champion of the national independence of an Eastern people against Western imperialists. Paradoxically the West ostracized until the very last months of his life (1938) the Turkish reformer who had abolished the caliphate and boldly introduced a secular state, the Swiss civil code, a real emancipation of women and a Latin alphabet – in sum, who had Westernized his country both profoundly and at speed.

This ostracism might have been justified by Kemalist Turkey's negative and sometimes cruel treatment of the non-Turkish races which were struggling for recognition in Asia Minor, but in fact these matters hardly worried the West which was harassed by its

BLACK SEA
CASPIAN SEA
Istanbul
Ankara
Baku
Mosul
Teheran
CYPRUS
Kirkuk
Beirut
Damascus
Tel Aviv
Amman
Baghdad
Benghazi
Alexandria
Basra
CYRENAICA
Suez Canal
KUWAIT
Cairo
RED SEA
QATAR
TRUCIAL OMAN
Mecca
HADHRAMAUT
YEMEN
Aden

THE MIDDLE EAST 1928

Foreign Colonies
Foreign occupation
Countries under British Mandate
Countries under French Mandate
Foreign Protectorates

traditional commitments and incapable after its victory of grasping all the aspects of the new Middle East. The allied arrangements of 1915–16, which were tainted by the self-interested grab for spheres of influence, were little improved by the treaty of Sèvres which outlined vague embryos of Armenian, Kurdish, etc. states alongside and at the expense of a fatally dismembered Turkey, and were as little viable. It might have been right and salutary boldly to create a mixed state or Kurdish–Armenian–Assyrian federation which, with the Ottoman yoke removed, could have constituted a zone of peaceful islamo-christian co-existence and East-West understanding on the borders of the Turkish and Arab worlds. Incapable of so novel a sweep of thought the West was led to sacrifice most of the national minorities which had put their faith in it.

These betrayals were chiefly the work of the Anglo-Saxons. In 1920 the American senate refused a mandate over Armenia and the Armenians were left with no future except development within the soviet orbit. When the Assyrians rose unsuccessfully against the Turks and had to flee, the British, who had hailed them in 1917 as 'our smallest ally', did give them refuge in Iraq and incorporated them in their levies, but they then used them on behalf of the Hashemite monarchy to subdue their Kurdish cousins. In 1924 the British confined themselves to a promise of a wide degree of freedom in the conduct of their purely local affairs but refrained from building anything in Iraq on their behalf, and after the Anglo-Iraqi treaty of 1930 they went no further than a platonic declaration to the League of Nations that if the Assyrians were willing to accept the point of view that they were destined to be citizens in a progressive state, they would be equitably treated. When their patriarch the Mar Shimun, head of the Nestorian community, made clumsy claims to a sort of mediaeval and tribal authority over the Assyrians, some of them fled to Syria in a fit of despair and their families left behind in Iraq were the victims of a horrible massacre (August 11th, 1933) of which the Iraqi authorities were the accessories if not the instigators. Deceived by British promises the Assyrian peoples were thenceforth doomed to dispersal and misery, a state from which they have not yet recovered.

The interest which the British momentarily showed in the Kurds was neither more lasting nor more fruitful. A mission to western Kurdistan in 1919 led by Major Noel had no sequel. At first the British favoured a modest form of autonomy for the Kurds in the south-eastern part of the Kurdish districts of Iraq where there were a medley of tribes in process of dissolution, feudal and religious chieftains of a traditional type and some urban groups attracted by nationalism and social progress. But they soon gave way before the obstacles in so heterogeneous a territory and were discouraged by the failure of the little principality of sheikh Mahmud at Sulaimaniya; they reverted to their prime concern which was to smooth away the difficulties facing the centralizing and Arab government in Baghdad. They therefore persuaded the Kurds, and even forced them by military operations, to be content with limited linguistic and administrative rights and an allegedly proportionate share of public offices. The existence of a Kurdish population was at least recognized in Iraq up to a point, whereas local Kurdish loyalties were repressed by violent or even cruel means in Turkey and by official pressure in Iran. Only in soviet Armenia and Syria did the Kurds, whose numbers were small in both those countries, meet with a really liberal and sympathetic attitude towards their culture.

In the matter of minorities, as in other fields, French policy in the Levant differed profoundly from British policy, for historical and psychological reasons which led to irreconcilable disagreement and sometimes to latent or open conflict. During the war of 1914–18 the French were too deeply embroiled on the western front to be able to send more than weak forces or infrequent missions to the Middle East. When the war was over they were forced to exchange the protective function which they had exercised throughout the Ottoman empire for a mandatory charge over a part of the Levant which was small enough to begin with and was constantly reduced by successive agreements. In the past they had had special contacts with the minorities and the intellectual precursors of Arab nationalism but they felt estranged from the Arab movement to the extent that it had found a different social ground, British patrons and a new, aggressive political tone. Moreover the French were slow to assess the potency of the new ideas which were spreading through the modern Middle East, and the pace of developments. They therefore conceived their mandate as a work of rational but progressive equipment and long-term education in administration and politics, to be conducted with a scrupulous and patient regard for local particularism. They were soon overtaken by events, although they had accomplished a task whose profound effects they did not always appreciate at the time.

Hence the distinction drawn by France between the nature and destinies of the two Levant states entrusted to French mandate, Lebanon and Syria. In the latter the French set up a series of districts which long retained their distinctive characters.

Grand Lebanon, created in 1920 and converted in 1926 into the Lebanese Republic, was constructed round the old autonomous nucleus of Mount Lebanon or Lesser Lebanon. The historical interdependence of Druzes and Maronites became the nucleus of a wider co-existence of various Christian and Moslem communities, no one of which constituted a majority and among which therefore minority problems properly so called did not exist. The proper allocation of public offices and responsibilities among these communities, and an electoral system which grouped voters of all communities on a common roll, produced in Lebanon's traditionally tolerant atmosphere a unique and original political balance.

The mistake of the French mandate was its failure to realize that Lebanon's level of development and its readiness to accept Western values and friendships justified a rapid emancipation which would have given France a unique opportunity to establish sound relations with a non-hostile Middle Eastern nationalism. But this nationalism was nearly always overlooked by the representatives of the French mandate. I myself have described elsewhere how the revelation of this nationalism took me by surprise in 1931 and I would like to quote my own confession by way of illustration:

> At this time I was discussing necessary reforms in Lebanon with a Beirut lawyer, an ambitious and resolute man with whom I was in general agreement. I felt that our conversation was a constructive one, when suddenly he pointed to the window and exclaimed bitterly, 'All this is useless. How can we change anything so long as our streets are patrolled by Senegalese soldiers?' For me these troops were the men who had helped to remove the Ottoman yoke and were now preserving law and order, but suddenly I saw that even with their rifles at the order they were an affront to the people of Lebanon.

The atmosphere in Syria was more tense from the beginning; also more complicated because of the lack of a single historic pole of attraction, the influence of neighbouring Arab countries and the existence of various dissenting Moslem or Christian minorities in the midst of a Sunni Moslem majority.

Circumstances unfortunately gave the mandate a violent beginning. On July 25th, 1920, French troops evicted King Feisal, who had been installed by the British and had shown no enthusiasm for French protection, from Damascus. The mandate was therefore regarded unfavourably by the nationalists, who raised an armed revolt in 1925 and started riots of decisive significance in the towns in 1936. For its part the mandatory régime set out to modernize the country; it retained the greater part (though not the whole) of the organic law passed by the Constituent Assembly in 1928, adding a few articles designed to entrench its own prerogatives and means of action; and it eventually found itself in almost permanent conflict with the nationalists over the question of Syrian national unity.

At the beginning the area entrusted to French mandate was divided by the mandatory into four states (Damascus, Aleppo, the Alaouites and the Jebel Druze) and the autonomous sanjak of Alexandretta. This division reflected local loyalties, the centrifugal and touchy attitudes of the dissenting islamic sects, and the rights secured by treaty to the Turkish minority. Surely, but from the nationalist point of view too slowly, the mandatory régime reduced autonomous powers while safeguarding minority rights; but on the other hand the settlement of Christian and Kurdish refugees from Anatolia in the Jazirah, Syria's easternmost province, created a new core of local loyalty strongly antagonistic to the centralizing policy of Damascus.

Nationalist pressures induced France to negotiate and in 1936 a treaty was signed which was in general similar to the Anglo-Iraqi treaty of 1930 but gave France greater prerogatives, especially with respect to the protection of minorities. (These prerogatives were subsequently expanded by an exchange of letters.) In spite of these reservations, and in spite of the notable concessions made by the Syrian nationalists in accepting them, French right wing opinion, which took a narrowly traditional view of the French mission in the Levant, conducted a powerful campaign against the 1936 treaty and the parallel treaty with Lebanon. The French government refrained from submitting the treaties to Parliament for an approval which was unlikely to be given and they remained dead letters. France thus lost the only opportunity of coming to terms with Arab nationalism in Syria.

Moreover Arab nationalism, it was increasingly clear, was becoming a movement which transcended the frontiers fixed at San Remo and which, independently of local movements such as those of the Syrian patriots (who were in any case susceptible to Hashemite influences), was spreading throughout the Arab world. It was thus discovering the deeper purpose which it had only temporarily shelved for tactical reasons. One of the Arab nationalist leaders, Shakib Arslan, who personally embodied the unification which was afoot, being a Lebanese Druze (presumably agnostic) who had become a Sunni Moslem and a Saudi

Arabian subject, was the author of an article published in a Damascus paper in January 1933 which contained these words: 'French opposition to partial unity should bring home to the peoples of the Syrian hinterland the need for a much wider field of action – Arab unity.'

CHAPTER 4

London curbs the Zionists

THERE WAS ONE complaint which the Arab nationalists could not level against the French, however: far from favouring any extension of Zionism to Syrian and Lebanese territory, France put every obstacle in the way. Britain was in a far more difficult position since it had both taken the initiative in establishing a Jewish national home in Palestine and was at the same time encouraging the Arab movement from an Iraqi base; and it tried to reconcile these opposites by on the one hand curbing Zionism in Palestine and denying it a political role and on the other hand creating a buffer and vassal state, Jordan, between Palestine, Iraq, Saudi Arabia and Syria.

At first Hashemite nationalism was not alarmed. It was reassured by the British who minimized the scope of the zionist experiment; and Hussein and Feisal in turn resigned themselves to the Jewish 'home' in which they may have seen no more than a new, more comfortable and safer ghetto, submerged in an Arab empire which would benefit from its industry and tax contributions. Not until January 20th, 1921, more than five years after the Hussein-MacMahon correspondence, did Feisal explain to the Foreign Office that in his view Palestine should be considered part of the promised zone of Arab independence.

Local opposition, which sometimes led to violence as in 1920 and 1921 at Jaffa and was fanned by more far-seeing Arab leaders such as the future Grand Mufti of Jerusalem, Haj Amin al-Husseini, was the work of an activist minority and had as yet little effect. For most Palestinian Arabs the arrival of Jewish immigrants who paid good money for virgin land of no apparent value and distributed high wages was by no means a calamity. The British administrators judged that in these circumstances economic prosperity for all and good government would work a political miracle, by which they meant a gradual flowering of political solutions of a new kind.

To Lawrence's dream of the Arabs as 'our first brown Dominion and not our last brown Colony' – a dream which had already been more or less frustrated by the intransigent claims of the Arab movement – was added a new dream in Palestine of a 'seventh dominion'[1] on Jewish foundations but bearable for Palestinian Arabs.

On July 1st, 1922, Winston Churchill, at that time Colonial Secretary, issued a statement which confirmed the Balfour Declaration and then went on to say that it did not 'contemplate that Palestine as a whole should be converted into a Jewish National Home but that such a Home should be founded in Palestine'. The statement proclaimed as the objective of this new and undefined entity in international law 'the further development of the existing Jewish community with the assistance of Jews in other parts of the world, in order that it may become a centre in which the Jewish people as a whole may take, on grounds of religion and race, an interest and a pride'. At the same time Britain gave the Arabs a number of assurances regarding their rights, their language and their culture, and affirmed the British intention to proceed with the establishment of self-government in Palestine.

The creation of a Jewish National Home in Palestine posed nevertheless two vital questions concerning a future Palestinian state, whatever form this might take. How far would such a home be endowed with para-governmental organs whose existence would to some extent entail a derogation of sovereignty? And did the Balfour Declaration's undertaking to welcome immigrants amount to an engagement to permit unlimited Jewish immigration to the extent of completely upsetting the communal balance in Palestine?

By the terms of the mandate itself an officially recognized

[1] This was the title of a book published in 1928 by the Labour Member of Parliament, Josiah Wedgwood.

Jewish organization was to co-operate with the Palestine administration. In this way the zionist organization and then the Jewish Agency set up offices in Jerusalem which, in particular, managed the Palestine Foundation Fund (a financial organization covering land settlement, education, immigration, public health, employment and religious affairs) and the Jewish National Fund which aimed to free the soil of Palestine by creating a national domain in the inalienable and undivided ownership of the Jewish people. Although many attributes of power (defence, foreign affairs, etc.) were missing from this pattern, it none the less contained the principal germs of autonomy and, what is more, was infused with a powerful creative urge.

This embryo could only develop through immigration, which was in theory limitless since every Jew had the right to be admitted to Palestine, but in practice and by agreement with the zionist organization it was governed and restricted by the Churchill declaration of July 1st, 1922, which stipulated that the volume of immigration must not be 'a burden upon the people of Palestine as a whole'. But the application of these arrangements, especially as events precipitated the migration of Jews from central Europe, provoked chronic and increasingly bitter conflict between the British administration in Palestine and the Zionists. In Jewish eyes the various measures taken by the British in the years after the first World War were inspired by the desire to soothe their Arab friends and allies and so improperly to limit the application of the Balfour Declaration, so far as was possible.

To the Zionists therefore the creation of the emirate of Transjordan looked like a fresh expression of this policy of divide and rule; at the least it showed the deadly skill, more often than not effective, of British manœuvres in the Middle East. The essence of these manœuvres, as has already been explained, lay in a master alliance with the Arab movement; but the British on the spot were too well aware of the cross-currents in the Middle East, and of the complexity of the commitments forced by circumstances on their government, to allow their actions to be determined by a single theme, however predominant. They regulated their activities without losing sight of the central theme but also without neglecting the pull of minor interests; these they then used, whenever possible, to further the pursuit of Britain's grand design.

Towards the end of 1920 Abdullah, son of Hussein, was ranging the steppes of Transjordan. He had been summoned to the throne of Baghdad by a congress of notables but the British did not intend him to occupy it and, disappointed, he cast an eye on the vacant throne of Damascus, from which Feisal had recently been driven by the French. It did not suit the British that Abdullah should provoke a dispute between the allies by attacking the French; on the other hand, it could suit them to have him firmly and securely settled in the vicinity of Syria, providing a place of refuge for Syrian dissidents and an example of an autonomous Arab power for disappointed Syrian nationalists to contrast with the strict provisions of the mandatory régime in their own country. A Hashemite state on this particular border would have the additional advantage of setting a solid buffer between the Saudis, whose relations with Britain were bad, and the sympathizers they might be tempted to seek in the neighbourhood of Damascus and Jerusalem. Finally, this arrangement would succeed in containing the zionist experiment and would create a sort of lock-gate between Iraq, where the tide of Arab nationalism was at its highest, and Palestine, where it was inopportune to allow it to rise.

And so on September 16th, 1922, the Transjordanian march was detached from Palestine in conformity with the prudently-worded general provisions of the mandate and excluded from the scope of the 'zionist articles' relating to the Jewish national home. It was turned into an emirate for Abdullah, given a separate government on May 25th, 1923, and linked by treaty to Great Britain on February 20th, 1928. Notwithstanding all these provisions, and yet with perfect discretion, Britain retained in Amman all the prerogatives of a mandatory power.

This conjunction gave the Arab movement under Hashemite

auspices those possibilities already described, at almost the very moment when Britain had to abandon the idea of a vassal kingdom of the Hedjaz under King Ali, this territory being annexed in 1926 to Nejd to form the kingdom of Saudi Arabia. The process also gave the Arabs the satisfaction of seeing the area originally marked out for the zionist experiment reduced in size. On the zionist side the loss of a field for expansion which could not be effectively appropriated for many years was offset by acquiring for neighbour an astute, clever and probably self-seeking Arab prince with whom there was the best available chance of some mutually profitable and peaceful settlement.

The creation of this equivocal principality is a suitable point at which to bring to an end this survey of the intermediate period which runs from the first World War to the years immediately preceding the second. The distinguishing feature of this period is the assertion of Arab nationalism – assertion rather than consummation. Many shortsighted observers were to seize on this obvious distinction and deny any genuine significance to the Arab movement, and this ill-founded denial was the great weakness of the Western policies of the period, London's alone excepted. Although the Arab national conflict was fought in these years in compartments determined by the state boundaries drawn by the major Powers; although the Arab conscience was slow to take shape and voice its claims in some of these territories, notably Palestine; and although many leaders of the Arab movement were still vacillating because opportunist; nevertheless a feeling of unity was beginning to emerge and in the movement thinkers were trying to inject this master-concept into the adventure, for men of vision could already discern the shape of things to come.

Where practised politicians frequently go wrong, an experienced sociologist may escape the pitfalls. In 1933 Robert Montagne, at that time director of the French Institute in Damascus, noted among the Arabs of the Middle East 'a profound unity of aspiration and direction and a close interdependence between groups. The Arab countries,' he went on in an article published under the pseudonym of Louis Jovelet, 'are confusedly striving for unity, for the realization of an "Arab nation". . . . The solidarity of the various states of Arabia, which has its limits and does not exclude serious domestic quarrels, is demonstrated by a glance at the local press in the Middle East, which spreads its net wide. It is also to be seen in a ceaseless coming and going and the ease with which people settle in one country or another; above all it finds expression in a common ideology which seeks . . . everywhere to arouse identical reactions in political, cultural or religious affairs. Thus an "Arab imperialism" is being born which seeks its inspiration in the past . . . or tries to link in the present . . . all the national movements which have arisen separately in the various countries of the Middle East.'

Having given this pertinent survey of the facts he outlined with exceptional insight the philosophy of this Arab design for living which, though still vague, was borne along by high ambitions. 'While with us the idea of a nation, however complex, takes comparatively precise geographical, ethnic, political and economic forms . . . in the Middle East the same concept is essentially diffused and nebulous and can be used to cover either very small groups or vast conglomerations. At the centre of the "nebula" is local loyalty, a feeling of belonging to a district like Lebanon or to one of the great provinces of Islam (Iraq, Syria in the larger sense of the word, the Hedjaz). In a less distinct form it appears as a belief in the unity of the race – the race which is one day to people the whole of the Arabian peninsula. Again, it is reflected in a faith in the historic and cultural unity of the peoples of Arab tongue and dialect from the Persian Gulf to the Atlantic, and finally it produces the vision of political unity throughout the vast extent of the Moslem world which, having adopted the religion of the Prophet, uses the "sacred language of God" (even if only for liturgical purposes). . . . When a Middle Easterner speaks of nationalism . . . it is almost always impossible to know which of the four aspects of the "nebula" he has in mind at the moment. . . . His "Arab fatherland" has at one time 5 million inhabitants (Syria, Palestine) and at another 15 million (Arabia). It can grow to 66 million when all the

Arabic speaking peoples are included and to 300 or 400 million to embrace the whole of Islam.'

In this analysis Robert Montagne was thinking primarily of the classic intellectuals of the Arab movement – Shakib Arslan (already mentioned) and Ihsan al-Jabri (a member of the Moslem upper middle class of Aleppo), editors of the monthly review *La Nation arabe* which had been published in Geneva from 1930. He says of them that they 'were concerned to uphold as much the cause of the Syrian nationalists (Syrian – Palestinian – Lebanese), as that of the Arabic speaking peoples, the cause of Islam and sometimes even the cause of the whole East against the West.' But at the same time he drew attention to the impassioned appeals of a coming man, the real prophet of the Arab movement, Abd al-Rahman Azzam Pasha. He attached particular importance to a powerful article by the future secretary-general of the Arab League which appeared in the first issue of the Jerusalem review *Al Arab* (August 27th, 1932) under the title of 'The Arabs, the people of the future'.

'While propaganda for Arab unity is taking shape,' wrote Azzam Pasha, 'and making its impact on timid and hesitant Arab peoples, those who are launching it cannot fail to perceive the importance of and good grounds for their efforts. . . . Arab unity is a present reality and a historical reality. . . .The fragmentation of the Arab nation into peoples and tribes is not a sign of dissolution or of falling vitality but simply one of the marks of ignorance and one of the manifestations of the impact of the Europeans on the east. But these divisions will not prevent the Arab nation from taking its rightful place. . . . If the Arab race prevails, then the finest qualities will likewise prevail. The Arabs' need for unity is not open to doubt, any more than is the world's need of the Arabs. Look therefore towards the nation of the future, the Arab nation.'

But as he spoke thus, the prophet of the 'Arab nation' seemed unaware that it was not alone in the field he claimed for it. There is no mention of zionism in his article and he had not yet recognized the irreconcilable enemy who would in the years to come focus the diffused enthusiasms of Arab sentiment on to Palestine and so give their propaganda concrete form and more concentrated force. For even Azzam Pasha was slow to identify the budding Israeli nationalism which was so gravely to challenge Arab nationalism in the 'twice promised' land and provoke a conflict destined to dominate the next two decades.

PART IV

THE PERIOD OF ARAB–ISRAELI TENSION (1936–55)

Chapter 1

The Arabs and the Axis

As has been explained, nascent Zionism was not at first regarded by the Arabs as a fundamental menace. There is hardly any exaggeration in the Jewish Agency's statement in March, 1939, that 'in the crucial years from 1917 to 1921 no Arab leader made any claim to Palestine on the basis of the MacMahon correspondence'.

In Palestine the earliest reactions against the intruders were not, properly speaking, nationalist; they seem rather to have been religious. The Jewish immigrants were of course not all practising Jews – far from it – and in any case they did not so present themselves, but their arrival touched what was Moslem in the Arabs, as though a forcible entry had been made, without divine warrant, into the *Dar ul Islam*, the House of Islam, the land of allegiance to Allah. It is no coincidence that the first person to speak out against the immigrants, and against the British who sponsored them, was an islamic jurist, the mufti Haj Amin al-Husseini. The British, in an attempt to neutralize this important personage, committed the great tactical blunder of trying to do so by augmenting his specifically Moslem responsibilities.

Apart from the isolated scrimmages in Jaffa in 1920 and 1921 Arab resistance, which stiffened by degrees, at first took the form of non-co-operation with the administration. The first serious incident (it accounted for 249 deaths) did not occur until the summer of 1929, in Jerusalem. It took place at the Wailing Wall, the last vestige of the Temple of Solomon, which was a sacred spot for Moslems as well as Jews since the horse, Burak, which carried Mahomet to heaven, had been tethered there. Once again the pretext was religious, but thereafter the contest became one of outraged feelings on both sides.

An islamic congress, sponsored by the mufti Haj Amin, met in Jerusalem in December 1931 to discuss ways of defending 'the second holy city of Islam' against Zionism. The programme of the congress was religious and cultural to begin with, but as it developed it became passionately political. Although the spectre of Zionism won some Christian support for Islam (particularly in Greek Orthodox circles) and although the leadership of the prayers was entrusted by the congress to a shiite, unity was never in sight. The mufti's enemies among the Palestinian Arabs were hostile; Turkey was critical of the 'use of religion for political ends'; there were no official delegates from Iraq or the Nejd, or from Egypt which looked askance at anything that might challenge the supremacy of the university of al Azhar. The congress failed to generate any practical action or to create an effective organization; all the same it made its mark by giving a jolt to opinion throughout the Arab world and by disseminating still further afield the emotions which the zionist danger had begun to arouse in Palestine.

The British government took some precautions of a legal nature. It stated officially that no more land in Palestine would be sold to Zionists, thus making immigration dependent on the extent to which land already in Jewish hands could be put to better use. This ban roused the Jewish Agency to indignation, for at the same time the rise of Nazism was driving a rising tide of human beings into the immigration offices.

It was by now unreal to measure the problem in material terms alone. The time had come to recognize that Zionism was predominantly a moral issue, though unmistakably a nationalist one as well. Yet few people saw this point. The few Western observers who did so were little heeded, let alone carried conviction. Not until about 1936 did the Arabs grasp the whole extent and nature of the danger that threatened them.

And yet the spirit of nationalism was manifest from the outset in each of those little collective settlements that were the advance guard of zionist colonization in Palestine – in each kibbutz. The youthful pioneers who laid out the roads, built the farms and dug the watercourses had come from lawyers' offices, artists' studios and libraries in central Europe; but in Palestine they accepted a collective discipline, a life of anonymity under canvas, the tedium of agriculture's monotonous round, and the lack of the usual intellectual resources. For their brief relaxation in the evenings they kept just a violin or a sketch book, a copy of the *Ethics* or the *Magic Mountain* by their camp beds, and when success rewarded their labours and the young colony balanced its accounts and could pay off its debts, they scorned to turn an assured credit balance into present comfort or entertainment. Bee-like they swarmed and started again further on.

Most of these pioneers were not practising Jews. In these little colonies a minute group of believers was often reduced to keeping watch for a pious visitor whose chance arrival might enable them to perform their rites and say their prayers in all due form. But the Mosaic tradition, like an ancient epic revived and translated into modern terms, determined the setting in which these people had chosen to live once more. It was not just anywhere, but in Zion, that the National Home had, after some hesitation, been established. Jewish law and socialist doctrine together shaped their institutions – such as the hereditary lease for 49 years by means of which the Jewish National Fund farmed out to settlers parcels of the inalienable real estate which had been recovered for the people as a whole. Thus did a nation once humiliated and dispersed renew the broken thread of its glorious history on the land that it was bringing back to life.

Essentially therefore Zionism was neither religious nor economic, but national. Leo Pinsker, the Jew of Odessa, had prophesied as much in 1882 when he wrote his *Auto-emancipation*. The important thing was not to rebuild the Temple, nor to create viable enterprises, nor even to found a sure asylum; the renascence of the Jews required 'the creation of a Jewish nationality, a firmly rooted people, the self-emancipation of the Jews, the acquisition of a land of their own where the nation might live among other nations and equal with other nations'. Zionists may be, and have been, divided about the need constantly to refer back to these principles, about the extent and shape of the venture, about the rhythm to be imposed upon it, about the opportunities or the dangers inherent in this way of proceeding or that. But these differences matter little. Allowing for all possible shades of opinion, the activity of each and all conduced to making Zion a sovereign reality; Zion was fundamentally national and nationalist.

But there was no room in the same 'twice promised' land for two different peoples each seeking to assert itself exclusively. The Arabs, too, feeling sundered by artificial frontiers, humiliated by clever imperialists and questing for an ideal, were striving no less than the Jews to give practical shape to the mystical conception of their unity. Destined, as they firmly believed, for early and complete emancipation, they could not be expected to concede sovereign rights to immigrants or allow their land to be used to build up the power and prestige of an alien people.

A bitter conflict between panarabism and Zionism was inevitable, though this fact was for some time obscured by manœuvres and scuffles, compromise and truce. In 1936 it broke out in disorders which were bloody, unatonable and hall-marked with cruelty and terrorism. This conflict was to dominate the affairs of the Middle East for twenty years.

At long last the British realized the full significance of the Palestine problem. On July 8th, 1937, a special commission of inquiry, under the chairmanship of Lord Peel, presented an instructive report. This document, which contained a thorough analysis of recent troubles, underlined among other things the considerable part played by 'external factors': the influence of the Arab movement in neighbouring countries, the example of nationalist successes elsewhere, the Anglo-Jordanian agreement of 1928, the Anglo-Iraqi treaties of 1930–32, and the Anglo-Egyptian, Franco-Syrian and Franco-Lebanese treaties of 1936. The report stressed the growth, as a counter to Arab nationalism, of a Jewish nationalism which was no longer to be satisfied with the halting institutions of the mandate. 'The National Home cannot be half-national. . . . Permanent minority status is not a national home. . . .' The report also showed how each community had in effect developed its own quasi-national institutions in the shape of 'parallel governments' – the Jewish Agency and the Arab Higher Committee affiliated to the Supreme Moslem Council. It rejected, as overtaken by events, the palliative solution of federating two Palestinian 'cantons', the one Jewish and the other Arab. It therefore recommended partition, that is to say, a complete and final severance; excluding a mandated zone to secure the neutrality and protection of the Holy Places it envisaged two sovereign independent states, the one Jewish and the other Arab, both linked by treaty with Great Britain.

Both sides protested, though with very different over-tones. Arab nationalists everywhere, regarding themselves as cut off from the Mediterranean by the plan, were extremely indignant, though the emir Abdullah was attracted by a prospect of extending his dominions and was therefore more restrained than his fellows. The Zionists refused to consider any political limitation on the immigration quota but were not indifferent to the blessing given to the idea of a Jewish state, however small. Both sides struck attitudes which were to remain the same, generally speaking, for ten years.

Moreover every attempt at partition – until the resort to arms in 1948 – ran into 'practical difficulties' such as those described by the very conscientious but disheartening Woodhead report of 1938; and the British cabinet, resolved (as it proclaimed in November 1938) to maintain responsibility for the government of the whole of Palestine, resorted to a succession of laboured and ephemeral palliatives.

Arab opposition, galvanized by the threat of partition, became both more precise and more general. A panarab parliamentary congress met in Cairo in September 1938 for 'the defence of Palestine', but it failed to achieve unanimity. Neither Saudi Arabia nor the Wafd in Egypt (not then in power) would be associated with its activities. And meanwhile circumstances gave Zionism a new and unforeseen impetus.

Adolf Hitler, however paradoxical it may seem, was one of

the principal benefactors of the Jewish National Home. He contributed more than any other man to the establishment of the state of Israel just as later he was to be its unwitting posthumous saviour, as shall be seen. From 1933 German and Austrian Jews began to flock to Palestine, impelled by premonitions of things to come. They contributed not only numbers but also their skills, their intelligence, their spirit of enterprise and their capital. For all its hatred the Third Reich was realistic and allowed the Jews to take their money with them provided it was reinvested in concerns that did business with Germany, and right up to the war there was in the Nazi consulate in Jerusalem a vice-consul (who had incidentally a Jewish mother) specially responsible for these matters.

In spite of these curious ramifications, of which they were hardly aware, the Arab nationalists regarded the Nazis as their natural allies and, soon, as a major source of comfort and support as well. Nazism was not merely assailing the Jews, whose Zionism made them the irreconcilable enemies of the Arabs movement. Better still, the Nazis were defying the Western begetters and supporters of the National Home that had been thrust into the Arab flank like a thorn and was beginning to fester. The traditional Moslem taste for an authoritarian form of society which combines 'religious' and 'national' emotions into a single driving force, as well as an innate respect for strength and a touch of romanticism – all these things combined to bring about an unwritten, but none the less real and effective, alliance between the Axis and the Arabs. Moreover world war was visibly approaching, and weighty and immediate anxieties were pressing upon Great Britain, the leading Western Power in the Middle East, and to a certain extent upon France too.

The measures taken by the future Allied Powers to meet these anxieties must next be briefly summarized. Mussolini's expedition against Ethiopia disturbed the Middle East the more because Italy, which had never concealed its vague but ambitious designs on the Anatolian coast and the Straits, simultaneously reinforced its garrisons in the Dodecanese and turned these islands into a sort of rear base. Thereupon the Western democracies concluded that the time had come to offer guarantees of security to all states concerned about the stability of the Middle East and so to form a Middle East defence association. Greece and Turkey joined the proposed pact. The settlement, in Turkey's favour, of the quarrel about Alexandretta certainly did no harm, although it understandably wounded the Syrians who were galled by the failure of their protecting Power to rally to their side. On the eve of war Great Britain, France and Turkey went so far as to conclude an alliance in good and due form; it was signed on 3rd September, 1939.

France abandoned for the immediate future the 'treaty policy' in the Levant states which it had failed to pursue to its logical conclusion. Acting upon articles which it had added to the organic statutes of both Syria and Lebanon, the French put the constitutional life of the two countries into cold storage and set up governments of civil servants which, much to their relief, were absolved of all responsibility for keeping order and feeding the civilian population.

Great Britain, too, tried to freeze the Palestine problem after fruitless efforts to get an Anglo-Arab-Jewish round table conference and putting out unproductive feelers in Iraq, Egypt and Arabia. London decided that the only course was to be more precise than before about restrictions on Jewish immigration and relegate the briefly glimpsed Jewish state to the distant future. A White Paper published on 17th May, 1939, proposed, at ten years' remove, a Palestinian state in which Arabs and Jews would jointly exercise authority; while the degree of co-operation required was being progressively built up, Jewish immigration was to be limited to a total of 75,000 persons over the ensuing five years.

The Zionists saw this scheme as a dire blow to their human resources, and regarded it as a renunciation of the Balfour Declaration. They felt entitled to circumvent the new regulations, which were by their standards iniquitous, and they organized clandestine immigration. All means were used, from the sabotage in a Palestine port of a ship carrying illegal immigrants (who had as a result to be admitted, though the British deducted their number from the authorized quota), to the dynamiting of immigration offices in order to retrieve old entry permits and use them again. The official ban was even applied during the war to Jewish refugees from Axis-occupied territories; 300 of these unhappy people, piled into the S.S. *Struma* and barred from the Promised Land, chose to scuttle their ship and drown themselves in the Black Sea rather than return to Bulgaria.

The exasperation engendered on both sides by such acts of desperation, and by violence and repression, led immediately after the war to ruthless anti-British terrorism, to which the British replied by methods no less grim. The terrible yet inspiring story can be read in *The Revolt* by Menahem Beigin, one of the leaders of Jewish resistance.

Yet however great their grievances against the British, the Zionists realized that the future of the National Home, and even its very survival, depended on the victory of the Western democracies. They therefore offered to make their contribution to the Western war effort and rendered distinguished service at the front within the narrow limits which the British, fearful for the future, allowed.

The Arabs for their part displayed at this juncture one of the psychological traits which was to persist and, once understood, explains the whole subsequent chain of events down to the present time. Their attitude was entirely governed by nationalist sentiment, by an exclusive concern with Arab interests, and by a daily increasing hatred of Zionism which they now saw as the greatest obstacle to Arab designs. From this point onward all Arab thinking and feeling was conditioned by the Palestine problem and nothing else. Nothing mattered except the national struggle; in every other contest they were to some extent neutral. They became wholly dominated by their national aims and regarded world affairs as, in a sort of way, non-existent; or rather, they took note of world affairs and judged them only in terms of their own particular conflict and national cause.

Was not their cause predominant? Abd al-Rahman Azzam Pasha, calling on the 'peoples of Arab tongue' to fight against ignorance and imperialism, had defined their ineluctable mission in ambitious and impassioned phrases which had made an indelible mark on their minds: 'By saving the Arabs, they shall save the whole world . . . over which materialism has spread its wings since the sun set on Arab culture. . . . If the Arab race triumphs, perfection will prevail, materialism will decline and the way of the spirit will take its place. And if the Arabs endow the world with the true way of life, they will have saved it from the misery in which it has been struggling and will have created it anew.'

Thus it is hardly surprising that the Arabs, convinced that their fight for independence and their search for unity were major movements of the age, treated the efforts and arrangements of the Powers as minor matters and regarded the imminent world cataclysm from their own particular point of view.

Arab nationalists had only three criteria by which to judge external events and regulate their own conduct: the dislodging of the foreign forces which had taken hold of Iraq, Egypt, Syria and Lebanon; the fight against Zionism which had thrust an even more noxious 'Western Presence' into Palestine; and the rejection of all those foreign influences which seemed to Arabs to be fomenting division in the Arab world and obstructing the grand design of liberation and unity.

Nor is it reasonable to upbraid the Arabs because they applied no moral criteria when passing judgment on the rival belligerents. They had at one time expected freedom at the hands of the Western Powers, with their democratic principles and parliamentary forms, only to see their expectations disappointed after the Allied victory of 1918; and they had been exposed to the lures of fascist and nazi totalitarianism which appealed to their own concepts of authority and the community. But above all they distrusted all foreigners whatsoever. They held them to be equally selfish; none was wholeheartedly devoted to Arab unity, neither Great Britain which had failed to serve the Arab cause to the end and had made itself hateful by hanging on to bases in Egypt and Iraq; nor France which protested its equal regard for all peoples but whose protection of minorities was suspected of being a cunning means to domination; nor even Germany, drunk with its own sense of mission and its racial superiority. Henceforward the Arabs would keep to themselves. They would choose friends and allies *ad hoc* (preferably from outside the Western Camp which seemed to them guilty of aggression against them) but would attach themselves to no cause, because to do so would be to betray their own, the only, cause.

This paroxysm of panarabism explains the attitude of the Arabs during the second World War, as it has continued to explain their neutralism in the conflict between the two post-war blocks. Anybody who fails to grasp this truth can have no fundamental understanding of the affairs of the Middle East and will always be baffled and led astray by passing events.

In 1939 therefore Arab national sentiment inclined to the Axis because it was against Zionism. But the challenge to the Allies was not made in Palestine, where the British had assembled a stiff array of military and police forces, but in Iraq, which the British had chosen to be the paladin of the Arab movement.

Immediately after the massacre of the Assyrians in 1933 King Feisal disappeared from the scene. This frightful deed, of which he learned to his astonishment while in Switzerland, shocked him deeply. Would not Iraq, which had so recently won its independence, be totally discredited? This fear was based on an exaggerated estimate of the tenderness of the Western conscience, but the Arab monarch, shattered by grief, died a few days later from a heart attack. His son and successor, Ghazi, was a young man of violent temper, mad about racing cars and speed; six years later he was killed driving at the very gates of his palace. Meanwhile he had allowed Iraq to be deflected from the prudent and patient Arab policy sponsored by Britain in order to pursue the lures of extreme nationalism. For a few months in 1936 Bakr Sidki, one of the instigators of the Assyrian massacres, was placed in power by a military dictatorship, and popular favour, deserting the wily Nuri al-Said who was tarnished by his British connections, swung to the energetic Rashid Ali el-Gaylani; this last was invested with some of the religious prestige of his ancestor Sidi Abd al-Qadir, the great saint of Islam who is buried in Baghdad and whose order, the Qadriya, extends its influence over the whole Moslem world.

In the first days of the war the grand mufti Haj Amin el Husseini left his precarious place of refuge in Lebanon, whither he had fled from Palestine, and established himself in Baghdad where the five year old Feisal II was under the care of his uncle and regent Abdul Illah, a loyal legatee of the ideas of Feisal I and a champion of the link with Britain. But the regent was soon forced to give office to Rashid Ali whose star had risen yet further with the arrival of the mufti and the support of the populace. The British were no longer in a position to oppose this disturbing turn of events but, relying on the treaty of 1930, they continued to use Iraq as a base for operations against the Axis on the borders of Egypt and Libya; they judged it safer to disembark troops from India at Basrah than at Suez. Yet this decision became the occasion for conflict between London, determined to keep all matters affecting the transit of troops in its own hands, and Baghdad, anxious that the passage of large units should be staggered so that no new division might disembark on Iraqi soil before its precursor had left (since otherwise Iraq could be reoccupied in force). The British refused to give way and on 2nd May, 1941, Rashid Ali's Iraq rose against them and against the party of their ally the regent.

Rashid Ali certainly had the general approval of the Nazis but it is less certain that they had agreed the date of a rising which they supported only feebly. Unknown to Baghdad, they were in the midst of their preparations for the Russian campaign and were not anxious to open a new and remote Eastern front. In these circumstances a small column, assembled with some difficulty in Transjordan, was easily able to recapture Baghdad, put Rashid Ali and Haj Amin to flight, and reinstate the regent.

Chapter 2

Britain and Panarabism

Great Britain had felt the blast of the broadside and reacted promptly. On the one hand the British took these steps, many of them thankless, that prevented the Middle East from swinging over to the Axis; on the other they simultaneously revived their policy of support for Arab unity, without undue anxiety about the contradictions in which their dual course might land them.

The British expeditionary force proceeded to invade Syria and Lebanon where the Vichy authorities had been unable to refuse facilities to German aircraft posting to Iraq or altogether to prevent the despatch of arms to the rebels. The Free French took care to associate themselves with the British expedition in order to safeguard French continuity in the Levant, but they were contending on unequal military terms with an ally who wanted not merely control of a theatre of operations but also a particular political bailiwick, and they were fairly soon ousted. In the same breath the British invaded Iran, where the government was displaying an ambiguous neutrality; nothing short of coercion could secure its co-operation in establishing contact through Iran between the British and the Russians, who advanced from the north to meet the British expeditionary force.

Turkey's case was more complicated. Associated with London and Paris by the treaty of 3rd September, 1939, the government in Ankara had hastened to redress the balance by negotiating a treaty on 18th June, 1941, with Germany. Its object was to preserve a stubborn neutrality (represented to each side as beneficial to its interests) and to get the most out of both sides without jeopardizing the destruction of Ataturk's work of modernization. Pro-German feeling, enhanced by hatred of Russia and certain panturanian designs, rose to a peak in Turkey on the eve of

Stalingrad, and it was not until 2nd August, 1944, that Ankara broke off diplomatic relations with Germany and 23rd February, 1945, that it issued a (purely formal) declaration of war. At any rate nothing vital was damaged by these shifts.

In Egypt, on whose western borders the British were locked in combat with the Axis, matters took a different course. Moslem feeling, which in Egypt was reinforced by reformism, was prompted by the Palestine drama into broadening local patriotism and turning it into a powerful Arab nationalism intent upon shaking off the British yoke and taking the lead in the common struggle. There was therefore nothing surprising in the fact that, from the first days of the war, the Axis enjoyed the favour of the Cairo populace and, discreetly, of the Egyptian government which even refused to declare war when the Italians invaded Egypt. Having learnt a lesson in Baghdad, the British took the bull by the horns in Cairo and on 4th February, 1942, applied sharp diplomatic pressure, backed by a military demonstration, in order to force King Farouk to appoint as Prime Minister Nahas Pasha, the leader of the Wafd and a supporter of Britain since the treaty of 1936. During the summer of 1942 the Cairo crowds were hopefully awaiting the arrival of Rommel's forces as liberators but the Wafd stood loyally by the British and supported British policy in Syria and Lebanon.

With these 'war services' to his credit, Nahas Pasha did not even wait for the end of the war before asking for a revision of the Anglo-Egyptian treaty. But the nationalists outbid him, and on 8th October, 1944, he was dismissed by the King who wanted to have a free hand *vis-à-vis* London in order to conduct a genuinely panarab policy, particularly on the Palestine issue. A new period of Anglo-Egyptian tension began.

Britain had at least succeeded, during the critical war years, in avoiding the worst in the political field. In the economic field the influential Middle East Supply Centre, established in 1941, had relieved governments of the heavy responsibility of finding food for their peoples and, while dealing very efficiently with this problem, had also given the Anglo-Saxons an inconspicuous and promising hold on material factors in the Middle East.

The British government was, however, well aware that these were not the only factors and that they weighed little in the balance against national emotions. So London, acting with boldness and imagination, took the first opportunity to initiate a new Arab policy, based once more on Iraq. British forces had barely entered Baghdad in triumph when Mr. Anthony Eden delivered a speech of the first importance at the Mansion House on the 29th May, 1941. 'The Arab world,' said the Foreign Secretary, 'has made great strides since the settlement reached at the end of the last war, and many Arab thinkers desire for the Arab peoples a greater degree of unity than they now enjoy. In reaching out towards this unity they hope for our support. No such appeal from our friends should go unanswered. It seems to me both natural and right that the cultural and economic ties between the Arab countries and the political ties too, should be strengthened. His Majesty's Government for their part will give their full support to any scheme that commands general approval.'

This speech was something of a masterpiece and cannot be too often or too carefully studied. Mr. Eden adroitly flattered the Arabs, expressly naming them 'friends' immediately after a revolt (which the legitimate government in Baghdad nevertheless severely repressed). He was careful to avoid all reference to what Britain had done for Iraq; on the contrary, he praised the progress made by the Arabs themselves. He did not confine his remarks to the relatively safe topics of culture and economics but boldly broached heady political issues. Yet his speech was not without prudence or guile, for he only promised to support plans that won general approval and so left open a wide range of choice and retained some freedom of manœuvre.

On this cue Nuri al-Said, who had just been reinstated in power in Baghdad, immediately took the stage with a plan which, designed to appeal both to Arab dreams and Iraqi ambitions, aimed at the unification of the Fertile Crescent. This area, which embraces the Palestinian, Syrian and Mesopotamian plains, constitutes a natural geographical and economical, if not an ethnic, unit; its political integration would be a first step along the road to Arab unity and a decisive move in Iraq's bid for primacy. Baghdad was to dominate the new state, whether its constitution were unitary or federal, and the Maronites of the Lebanon and the Zionists of Palestine were to have limited autonomy as protected minorities – a prospect little calculated to please them. Moreover, this recurrent plan for a Greater Syria, however attractive to the hard-headed merchants of Aleppo, was always suspect in Damascus where pride vies with local sentiment and where quite different ideas of Arab unity were entertained.

In any event Iraq helped Britain to stimulate in Syria and even in Lebanon a revival of Arab nationalism which led to the demise of the French mandates. But Egypt took a hand as well and, as we have seen, set about displacing Iraq as the leader of panarabism even before the war ended. Power was given to men untainted by the faintest collusion with the West, and the cause of Palestine was adopted with the extremism that alone appeals to Arab hearts and without any regard for Britain's difficulties.

It was in Egypt that, in the autumn of 1944, Arab unity was endowed with its first institutions. On October 7th, Syria, Lebanon, Transjordan, Saudi Arabia and Yemen joined with Egypt in signing the protocol of Alexandria. This document, which provided a blueprint for the future Arab League and guaranteed the independence and the territorial integrity of Lebanon, stressed the importance of the Palestine problem and pledged support in general terms for the Palestinian Arabs. The treaty of the Arab League was signed by the same states at Cairo on 22nd March, 1945. 'In response to public opinion' this organization aimed at 'the strengthening of the relations between the member states and the co-ordination of their policies.' The League was equipped with a secretariat, established in Cairo and directed by the fiery Egyptian political writer, Abd al-Rahman

Azzam Pasha. Its Council consisted of representatives of all its member states and its decisions were binding only if unanimous.

This arrangement was the outcome of second thoughts about individual interests, and of consequent nervousness about the federal formula adopted at Alexandria; it was to prove the organization's greatest weakness. But it must be stressed that this organic defect was wilful, especially on Egypt's part. M. Marcel Colombe, one of the shrewdest experts on the modern Middle East, has written: 'The fragmentation of political authority enshrined in the charter of the League crowned Egypt's dearest wishes.' Or, in the words of a British observer, in the League the Arab states provided a living-room for the idea of unity, preserving the bath water but throwing out the baby.

From the outset, the Arab League constituted a platform for spreading the gospel of Arab unity throughout the Middle East and enhancing the diplomatic weight that the Arabs carried in the world beyond; it was this rather than an amalgam of forces under single management. Moreover, although meetings were held in the various Arab capitals in turn, the location of its permanent organs in Cairo marked an important gain for Egypt. In fact Egypt lost no time in using the League for its own purposes. The Egyptians conveniently forgot both that the British had always encouraged Arab unity and that the vital problem in the Arab world was the Palestine crisis which had now reached its bitterest point. Egypt used the new organization against the British not, primarily, on account of Palestine but because it wanted to be rid of the last British strongholds on its soil, notably the garrisons in the Suez canal zone.

Therein lay one of the reasons for the ineffectiveness of Arab action in the new phase of the Palestine crisis which opened in earnest immediately after the war. Another reason was the appearance of the United States on the scene, a very important factor which must be considered next.

CHAPTER 3

The Palestine explosion

THE UNITED STATES, which had been undecided in 1941 and was still hesitant in 1943 even in face of the Russian threat to the Balkans, had by 1945 won the war, decided where the morrow's danger lay, taken the measure of the world and assumed its responsibilities. In the Middle East it saw one obvious task – defence against the Soviet block as a part of the defence of the West.

This is tantamount to saying that the Americans were fated to suffer the most serious misunderstandings in their dealings with the Arab world. But they failed to see their danger. On the contrary, events conspired to give them confidence: the rapid development of their oil interests in Saudi Arabia, the exhaustion of the British who pressed them to take over in Turkey and the Balkans, the eagerness of numerous Middle Eastern states to have American aid and advice, and the impetus of Zionism sanctified by memories of Nazi crimes and warmly supported by the Jews of the United States. Finally there were the hesitations of the U.S.S.R. which failed in 1945 to sustain its claims to Kars and Ardahan or to press the Straits question and then in 1946 abandoned its venture in Azerbaijan and withdrew its troops from northern Iran.

The Americans embarked on their task almost naïvely and without realizing that it was beyond their powers. 'These contradictory pledges' (given by the President to the Arabs and Zionists in 1943–5) 'were already implied in the American assumption of partial responsibility for resolving the deadlock to the mutual satisfaction of all concerned.' So wrote an excellent analyst, Mr J. C. Hurewitz, in his book *The Struggle for Palestine* (p. 214). The very first American attempts at a solution ran up against insoluble dilemmas and against a split in opinion at home, not only among the public but between the authorities. The State Department was opposed to President Truman when, brushing aside moderation and compromise, he endorsed on 4th October, 1946, the Jewish Agency's claim to 'a viable Jewish state in control of its own immigration and economic policies, in an adequate area of Palestine'.

On 14th February, 1947, the British, weary of bearing single-handed the brunt of a confused and cruel revolt which forced them to fight Jews and Arabs alike, decided to transfer the Palestine problem to the United Nations. After several attempts the General Assembly produced a partition plan with obvious imperfections on 28th November, 1947. Jerusalem was to be placed under permanent international trusteeship and two states were to be established, one Arab and one Jewish, both independent though linked economically, and each consisting of three pieces of territory connected by precarious corridors.[1]

The Jews accepted the plan as the best obtainable in the circumstances; at least it enabled them to build a state and they were content to postpone improvement of its shaky foundations. But the Arab states rejected the plan and the Americans had to acknowledge inability to enforce this international attempt at a solution, whereupon they were denounced by the Jews for shirking their responsibility and capitulating to Arab claims.

So the Americans, like the British before them, and more swiftly, failed to solve the Palestine problem despite the excellence of their intentions, their (possible naïve) generosity and their power. They were slow to realize that this was no ordinary problem. It should not have been treated (and still should not be treated) as solely a matter of national interests and human passions, but as a question of the Promised Land, any solution of which must be based on a charter for the Holy Places. Islam and Judaism, as well as Christianity, possess in Palestine shrines so dear to them that the peoples holding these monotheistic beliefs should be capable of sacrificing some of their political

[1] See map opposite.

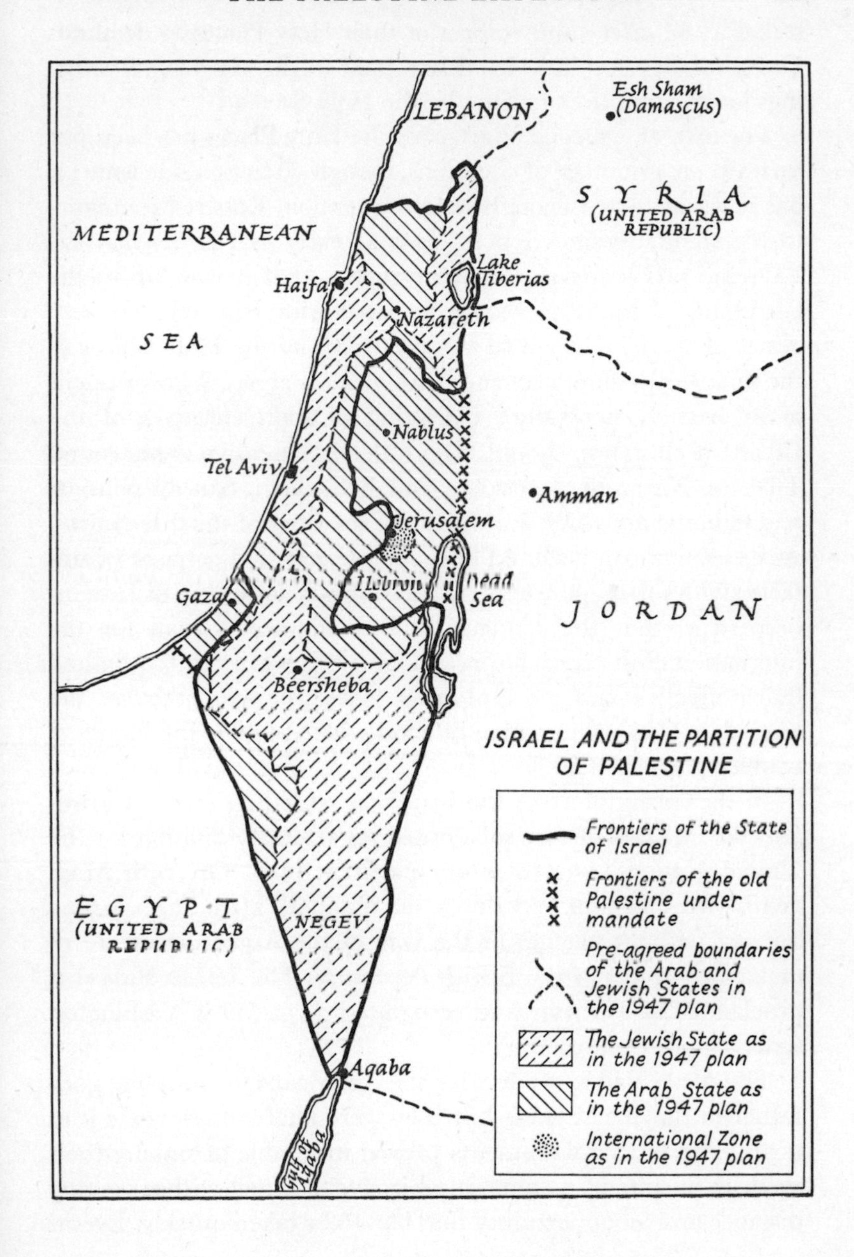
LEBANON
Esh Sham
(Damascus)
SYRIA
(UNITED ARAB
REPUBLIC)
MEDITERRANEAN
SEA
Lake
Tiberias
Haifa
Nazareth
Nablus
Tel Aviv
Amman
Jerusalem
Dead
Sea
Gaza
JORDAN
Beersheba
EGYPT
(UNITED ARAB
REPUBLIC)
NEGEV
Aqaba
Gulf of
Aqaba
ISRAEL AND THE PARTITION
OF PALESTINE
Frontiers of the State
of Israel
Frontiers of the old
Palestine under
mandate
Pre-agreed boundaries
of the Arab and
Jewish States in
the 1947 plan
The Jewish State as
in the 1947 plan
The Arab State as
in the 1947 plan
International Zone
as in the 1947 plan

stakes if the safety and respect of their Holy Places so demand. Unfortunately too little heed was paid to the considered warnings issued from time to time by the Holy See.

The idea of a special charter for the Holy Places has been put forward on a number of occasions, though often as a side issue; it has never attracted enough serious attention. Robert Montagne, to his credit, reminded politicians as early as 1947, when the Palestine problem was still manageable, that it was 'up to the Christians of today to reconcile Israel with Ishmael'. He suggested that 'the concept of the protection of the Holy Places of the three faiths should cover extensive peace zones. A government of an entirely new kind, consisting of representatives of the Christian churches, should keep order in extensive zones round Tiberias, Nazareth, Jerusalem and Bethlehem, ban all political and national activities, and facilitate the work of the three faiths. As its secular arm it should have an international corps of volunteers and a mixed police force.' [1] But it was not until 9th December, 1949, that the United Nations adopted a plan for the internationalization of Jerusalem, and this was both too limited to be effective and too ambitious to be put into practice. Yet some day, God willing, men of good will may solve the Palestine conflict along such lines.

In the spring of 1948 the issue was settled by force of arms, and the fortunes of war substituted an arbitrary division for the United Nations' unsatisfactory partition plan. On 15th May, 1948, Great Britain laid down the mandate after due warning but not without placing in the way of the Arabs the means of making the most of the British departure. The Jewish state was proclaimed at Tel Aviv and recognized *de facto* by Washington sixteen minutes later.

The Arabs will never forgive the Americans for standing godfather to the Jewish state but they were unable to strangle it at birth. The Arab governments proved incapable of sinking their rivalries in spite of a common objective, a target within striking distance and an opportunity that had to be taken quickly. Events

[1] *Le Monde*, 24th August, 1947.

in the second half of May suggested that the other Arab states wanted Transjordan, the best armed among them, to take the field alone and so exhaust its resources that after victory it would be unable to have its own way. The Arab Legion took Nablus, Samaria and Hebron and pushed on to the heights of Latrun whence Tel Aviv and the sea were visible only a few miles away. But in order to take the old city of Jerusalem the Legion had to fight a long and exhausting battle, and it failed to capture the new town and the suburbs which were strongly held by the Israelis. These last, by an extraordinary upsurge of the national will, instantly and miraculously fused into a single army all the clandestine forces hitherto controlled by separate movements – the quasi-official Haganah, Beigin's Irgun and the merciless Stern Gang. The Jewish Army was born at the same moment as the Jewish state and became at once a power in the land.

From that moment it was too late for the Arab forces to do anything effective. Their fate was that of the three Curiatii who were defeated in turn by the last of the Horatii – but without the redeeming feature of wounds before. Iraq saw what was happening in time and, using the evergreen excuse of a Kurdish rising, withdrew its troops almost before they had had time to become engaged. The Syrian army, having seized one or two frontier posts, was content with this token success. The Lebanese army merely staged a demonstration. Operations were interrupted by truces imposed by the United Nations, and by the time the Egyptian army joined the battle it was far too late; Egyptian units, poorly supported by their supply services and badly handled by the high command, fought in vain. But in the heat of battle some of the officers drew bitter conclusions about the causes of their defeat. Among them was Gamal Abdel Nasser.

The Arab states were forced to resign themselves to the existence of the state of Israel but they refused to recognize it. Iraq, having no common frontier with Israel, kept up the fiction of a state of war. The other governments concluded armistices under the auspices of the United Nations which sent an international corps of observers to man the demarcation lines, although more often than not they were powerless to prevent raids, incidents and bloodshed on both sides.

The Arab states regarded their defeat as temporary. During the armistice they recovered, if somewhat negatively, the solidarity that they had failed to establish in the campaign, and they armed themselves with two weapons with which they expected to be victorious sooner or later.

The first of these was the blockade of Israel. This tiny state, with a modern economic and social structure, but inadequate food production, with exportable commodities such as citrus fruits and with a fair but improving industrial capacity, had to trade to live. The Arab blockade cut it off from its natural markets in the East and, in defiance of the law, closed the Suez Canal and Gulf of Aqaba to goods destined for the Asian and African countries round the Indian Ocean.

On top of this Israel was obliged by its very nature to gather in all Jewish refugees who wanted to come. It had already received the Jews from Yemen, a simple-minded but sturdy people, coming of their own free will and easily assimilated in spite of their oriental and mediaeval character; and now it had to take in Jews from Iran and Iraq, expelled against their will on trumped-up charges of disloyalty. Most of the latter were office workers or urban tradespeople, middlemen of the type found throughout the Levant, who did not find employment easily in the pattern of Israeli society. With the best of its young people guarding the truce lines and an influx of unusable immigrants into the reception camps, Israel experienced the paradox of simultaneous unemployment and a shortage of labour.

In spite of heroic efforts and remarkable austerity Israel's national economy had a difficult start. In the first year imports exceeded exports by seventeen to one, and six years later the ratio was still about three to one. The new state would soon have been strangled if it had not had help from outside, sometimes of an unexpected kind. This included funds raised all over the world by the Jewish Agency, government and private aid from the United States, investment by American financiers taking a gamble on this vigorous young country, and finally funds from the Federal German Republic paid by way of reparations to the Jewish community for Nazi crimes. Once again Hitler was a benefactor, this time a posthumous one, of Israel.

Resources of this kind were, however, extremely unreliable. Vigorous Arab reactions caused Bonn to pause before persisting in its generosity, for fear of losing its trade with the Arab world. But boycott of Germany required a unanimous decision of the Arab League, and a skilful manœuvre, doubtless instigated by Tel Aviv and designed to appeal to Egypt's self-interest, persuaded Cairo to withhold its vote. There was another alarm when the Jews in the United States became afraid that their links with Israel might, by some MacCarthyist twist, be construed as incompatible with loyalty to the Union; they recovered confidence only slowly, and then not completely. Finally, the Israeli government had its worries about the policy of the State Department, soon to pass into the custody of Republicans anxious for better relations with the Arabs. Within Israel the socialist majority in the government had to face the disapproval of its more active supporters because it joined forces with liberal elements whose assistance was indispensable in securing foreign aid and support.

Israel was therefore forced to live dangerously – economically and socially, politically and strategically – but it was invigorated by this harsh climate and it survived and defeated the manifold dangers of the Arab blockade.

The Arabs had a second and no less redoubtable weapon against Israel: the Arab refugees from Palestine.

The story of these unhappy people is cruel and obscure. Panic seized the Moslem population of Judaea when certain Jewish elements massacred the inhabitants of Deir Yasin, near Jerusalem, in the chaos of early May 1948. Was this massacre the deed of a few fanatics or was it premeditated with the object of starting an exodus? In any case there may have been Moslem leaders ready to encourage the flight (believing it to be only temporary) in order to clear the field for the Arab armies that were to join forces against Israel. Whatever the truth, by the time of the armistice more than 500,000 Arabs from the territory of the new Israeli state were thenceforward refugees in the neighbouring Arab countries. Israel allowed a few Arab town-dwellers to return but refused with good reason to allow the bulk, hostile and potential members of a fifth column, to return to the land of which there was little enough for the Jewish immigrants.

The Arabs for their part proclaimed that the refugees had an inalienable right to return to their ancestral homes and refused to allow them to be settled elsewhere, even provisionally, for fear of giving the impression of yielding. So far from setting themselves to alleviate the lot of the refugees, the Arabs kept them in distress but ready for use, like a weapon. They were to be alike a threat to Israel, a warning to moderate Arab governments which might be tempted to waver, and a worry and a reproach to the conscience of the West. They even became a charge upon the West, since the refusal of the Arabs to establish them in the Arab states, or to give them land or work, meant that they were kept idle and relegated to camps where their numbers were steadily increased by natural processes and their needs could only be met by outside help. Relief was provided through a special United Nations' agency and was paid for almost exclusively by the West (particularly the United States), which reaped as its reward the undying hatred of the refugees who were taught by ceaseless propaganda to saddle the West with all their woes.

In spite of this hatred, or perhaps because of it, the United States endlessly sought a solution that would bring relief to the refugees and be acceptable to everybody else. One solution put forward was the harnessing of the waters of the deep valley of the Jordan, a project to be undertaken by all the riparian states along the lines successfully practised by the Tennessee Valley Authority; this was designed to irrigate much needed land and produce manifold other economic benefits for the states involved.

But this was mere repetition of the mistake of the British who had imagined in their day that they could bring Arabs and Jews together by making them partners in prosperity. Given the failure of the British in this direction and the inflamed passions of the time, the American plan was bound to be suspect. Aware of the difficulties President Eisenhower played out all his trumps. He despatched a personal representative and chose for this task Mr. Eric Johnston, a patient and discerning man who had earned an outstanding reputation as a mediator in the cinema industry in Hollywood. But the man who had succeeded in reconciling the whims of stars with the demands of producers failed, in spite of patient journeys year after year, to get the Arab riparian states to accept a plan which would make them rich but would also rob panarab passions of their pabulum.

These passions, accentuated by the bitter experience of the Palestine war, were more active than ever in the Arab soul. Behind the façade of political institutions, established social systems and accumulated fortunes they were beginning to re-fashion the more important states. The failures in Palestine started a great internal revolution whose import and extent only gradually became apparent.

This revolution was inspired and directed by Arab officers who were aware of the disasters they had suffered but were also convinced that the responsibility lay entirely with governments. Most of them came from the middle class, were close to the people and their needs, and knew more than most of their fellow citizens (including political leaders) about the exigencies of the modern world, the urgent need for reforms and the importance of personal integrity.

The first to rebel was a Syrian colonel, Husni Zaim, a picturesque and loyal military type, of Kurdish and Turkish rather than Arab origins, who had received his military education on French lines. On 30th March, 1949, without bloodshed, he ousted a government which seemed to him unworthy of its charge. Once in power he displayed a rough paternalism which found favour with the people but he failed to win over the nationalist political groups. Bent before all else on Syrian independence and distrustful of Baghdad, he tried to reinsure to the south. On 25th June he declared that 'Syria relied on the support of Egypt and Saudi Arabia and constituted with them the Cairo-Damascus-Riyadh triangle'. But after no more than 37 days he was brutally murdered by a small military group of local pro-Hashemite fanatics.

A few months later Colonel Adib Shishakli staged a third Syrian coup. Shishakli was a better politician than Zaim and held power for four years in a swirl of changing circumstances. By the time that he allowed himself to be forced out by a military clique on 27th February, 1954, rather than shed blood, he had made a significant contribution to the development of Syria. The political importance of the various communities had been reduced, American Point Four aid had been refused, some social progress had been set in train; last but not least, pan-arabism had been encouraged in consort, significantly, with a new Syrian nationalism. Syria was ripe for an upsurge of the forces of the Left and at the elections of September 1954 the Baath (the Socialist Arab Renaissance Party) won its first successes – soon to be increased.

Unlike the Syrian coups, the revolution which occurred in Cairo on 26th July, 1952, and swept away a corrupt monarchy and ruling aristocracy was not the work of soldiers alone. The Moslem Brotherhood, a fundamentalist Moslem sect, played an important – perhaps, if we are to believe its members, a dominant – part in it. But it was the 'free officers' who gave it its direction and impulse. These honest soldiers had thought over the Palestinian fiasco and come to the conclusion that the blame lay not simply with the high command but also with the government and monarchy. They introduced into the movement, with the least possible violence, a reform programme which won them enthusiastic popular support.

The first head of this new Egypt was the fatherly general Mohammed Neguib, but after eighteen months he made way for the more incisive figure of Colonel Gamal Abdel Nasser. The parts later played by this man in Arab and international affairs must not be allowed to obscure the fact that Colonel Nasser's first vocation, expressed in a not particularly brilliant but characteristic pamphlet *The Philosophy of the Revolution*, was that of a social reformer. Authoritarian certainly, but in tune with the modern world, sincerely anxious to help the humbler classes and in this respect more truly their friend than his nationalist and Wafdist predecessors – at heart Nasser wanted to be the protagonist of agrarian reform. Baulked by lack of funds and skills and by the procrastinations almost inevitable in such a venture, he failed to achieve the signal successes of his dreams, but he was at least able to deal some hard knocks and Cairo's underprivileged will never forget the sight of a pasha in convict's clothes on his way to hard labour for having resisted the partition of his estates. The ambitious reclamation plans in the model Liberation Province – the *Tahrir* – have not been really successful.

Thenceforward Nasser, while laying the blame for these failures on obstinately imperialist obstruction, began to ponder on the great plan for a high dam at Aswan to provide the vast resources needed for modernizing Egypt. His genuine endeavours, albeit unsuccessful, were advertised by excellent propaganda and won him widespread sympathy among the masses throughout the Arab world who were either ignored or ill-treated by reactionary governments amongst which were to be found the allies and vassals of the Anglo-Saxon West.

These tremors in the vast and fabulous land of Egypt did more than Syria's confusing coups to start the invisible crumbling of the Middle East. Nasser was cast for a Middle Eastern Garibaldi long before the events of 1956 stamped him on the fevered Arab imaginations as a Bismarck, the champion of unity in the making. Waves of unrest, the prelude of the Middle East's internal revolution, spread from the Baghdad populace (on the move since November 1952) to the Arab refugees (always in ferment) and the budding proletariats bunched round the oil installations and preparing the ground for the first strikes on the shores of the Persian Gulf. Such was the fruit of the Palestine drama of 1948 which had been the first cause of the military risings against the rule of the privileged and against government by pashas.

Chapter 4

Arab neutralism and Western defence plans

THESE EARLY SIGNS of upheaval in the Middle East deserved greater attention than they got at the time. Seen in conjunction with the extensive Arab grievances, they revealed the existence among the Arabs of a spiritual unity which enabled them to work together effectively for the first time. But ever since the end of the second World War the West had failed to keep touch with the Middle East as it had been wont to do. The points of contact had become fewer. Germany and Italy had been excluded by their adversaries and France by its allies. Only the Anglo-Saxons remained and their position was anything but straightforward.

The British enjoyed the advantages of long experience, an incomparable knowledge of the Middle East, and long tried – if somewhat antiquated – political methods. On the other hand they resented the general attenuation of their powers and they made up their minds to hold only vital positions in the future: political influence in the Hashemite kingdoms, with a finger in the Arab movement; an assured supply of sterling oil on the Persian Gulf; and, in discreet reserve, their traditional vassals and possessions on the periphery of the Arab peninsula. This policy of 'limited commitment' made them the associates of reactionary governments on the wane, and this was the great weakness of the system. On the other hand their abandonment of the Palestine mandate in 1948 was not a sign that they underestimated the primordial importance of the Arab-Israeli conflict but on the contrary a measure of their appreciation of it. They took the view that they must shed some of their load in the Middle East, but this was too simple a solution and it helped to lead them a few years later into the fatal impasse of the Baghdad Pact.

The Americans hastened to take the place of the British

whenever possible, but they inherited neither Britain's experience nor its farsightedness. Nor did they appear to have correctly judged the vital importance of the Arab-Israeli conflict, either at the outset in their ardent pro-Zionism or later in their haste to get on better terms with the Moslem states; they were quite unable to find their way about among the popular and unitary currents of an Arab nationalism which they underrated. It was on the contrary the complexities of the Middle East that struck them and they were bemused by the contradictions, dissensions and apparently irreconcilable feuds of the various states, and led astray by the notion that they could make a friend, even an ally, of each state in turn – or at least persuade it to keep out of a hostile coalition – by consulting its particular needs and wishes.

American aid to Turkey (substantial from 1947) and the sort of mediation offered to Iran in the oil dispute fell outside the Arab area, but within it the services and subsidies dispensed by the Americans, notably under Point Four, rarely seemed to evoke gratitude. In local opinion these gifts were not disinterested and they were contrasted with the help – more important in Arab eyes – given to Israel. Finally, the nationalists did not fail to note the discreet renewal by Saudi Arabia on 18th June, 1951, of the right to use the air base at Dhahran which had been created as a staging point to the Far East during the war. They concluded that the Americans were only interested in establishing themselves in the Middle East in view of a war against the U.S.S.R. into which everybody would be dragged.

It cannot be denied that from the way they went about things in the Middle East the Americans showed themselves very ill informed about the mentality of this part of the world. In particular they treated the Arab-Israeli problem on a par with every other Middle Eastern problem and in terms of their own preoccupations which, since the only thing they had in mind was a world war between East and West, were of a different order.

The American failure in the Middle East and the continuing bitterness of the crisis down to the present day were due essentially to this one cause. Having failed to see to the heart of the matter the Americans dispersed their efforts and proceeded from one strange contradiction to another. They disappointed Israel and offended the Arabs; they neglected the fundamental wishes of the Arab peoples while offering their governments material aid which was accepted and as soon denounced by public opinion as derisory or dangerous. In the end they tried to impose their own political concepts, and though they may have been justified in doing so by the world situation, their motives were far too foreign to the area to be apposite to it and to secure the necessary degree of local support. These were the principal factors in the West's misadventures, which must now be recounted.

The disorganization among the Arabs, which reached a peak in the winter of 1948–9, suggested that nothing could be built up in the Middle East except by outsiders. The Arab defeat was followed by one of those bitter periods when politicians are moved by contrariness and hatred rather than any feelings of brotherhood and solidarity.

The members of the Arab League were at each other's throats over the Arab remains of Palestine, although there was little enough left to quarrel about. Haj Amin presided over an Arab Palistinian government in the narrow Gaza enclave occupied by Egypt. The old city of Jerusalem, Nablus and Hebron with the surrounding countryside were simply annexed by Abdulla who thereby became King of Jordan.

This clever but over-ambitious prince won a Pyrrhic victory and in the end it doomed him. The annexation of this part of Palestine, together with the influx of refugees, distorted the balance of his mediaeval bedouin emirate and laid it open to the play of Arab passions. Adjudged a traitor to panarabism, he was done to death on the 20th July, 1951, by Cairo fanatics in the al-Aksa mosque in Jerusalem. The Jordanian court which sat in judgment on the crime found that a nephew and intimate counsellor of the grand mufti, Musa al-Husseini, was one of the principal instigators and sentenced him to death.

Under the spur of the enlargement of Abdullah's domains Hashemite ambitions soon reappeared and Baghdad, where the

Fertile Crescent plan was never far beneath the surface, proposed to Amman a military alliance as a first step. Cairo at once took fright at the prospect of losing the leadership of the Arabs and in order to check the Hashemite scheme went one better and proposed a general Arab defence pact. No member of the Arab League felt able to demur; the pact was signed on 13th April, 1950, but delays in ratification and reservations made by some of the signatories showed how far the Arab governments were from forming even a purely consultative military organization of any practical value.

The Arab Defence Pact was one of a number of sentimental or theoretical unification plans which the Arab League produced in plenty under the auspices of politicians like Hassan Hakim of Syria and Fadhi Jamali of Iraq – schemes principally designed to promote the interests of their sponsoring states under cover of Arab ideals.

Moreover, since any step towards a Hashemite alliance was a threat to Syria and Lebanon and a worry to Egypt and Saudi Arabia, the Arab Defence Pact was meaningless unless it were directed against Israel. To the Western Powers the time seemed to have come to try to put some limit to the chaos in the Middle East, even if they could not put an end to it. This was the aim of the tripartite declaration (by the United States of America, Great Britain and France) of 25th May, 1950: 'The three governments recognize that the Arab states and Israel all need to maintain a certain level of armed forces for the purpose of ensuring their internal security and their legitimate self-defence and to permit them to play their part in the defence of the area as a whole. All applications for arms or war material from these countries will be considered in the light of these principles.' The Western Powers, reaffirming their declarations of 4th August, 1949, opposing 'the development of an arms race between the Arab states and Israel', sought disclaimers of aggressive intentions from any state in the area asking for arms and condemned any use of force and any violation of frontiers or armistice lines undertaken or planned by any Middle Eastern state.

The tripartite declaration was certainly sound in its concern for the preservation of peace and stability in a region where these were threatened, but it was bound to annoy the Arab states; they rejected it on 21st June on the grounds that it implied the recognition of Israel and hardly paused to note that withal it paved the way for associating them with the general defence of the area.

Yet this was what the United States had definitely decided to do. The Americans even took the Arab Defence Pact to be a blueprint for a defence organization, similar to Nato and capable of becoming in time an extension of Nato. Turkey, anxious to draw every possible material advantage and guarantee from its military association with the West, had just won its way into the Atlantic Pact. Would it not be a good idea to make Turkey a geographical link between the two systems and attach it to a Middle East Defence Organization (M.E.D.O.) which would be provisioned by the West and have its centre in Egypt?

Unfortunately this plan betokened a complete misreading of the state of affairs in the Middle East. Iran had just succeeded in shaking the indirect tutelage of the Anglo-Iranian Oil Company by nationalizing the company's concession; Egypt believed that the time had come to stab at Britain while it was staggering under the blow from Iran, and on 8th October, 1951, Nahas Pasha unilaterally denounced the Anglo-Egyptian treaty of 1936 and unleashed a guerilla war against the British garrisons in the Suez canal zone, who retaliated smartly.

But the Americans, unperturbed, pressed on with their strategic plans. On 13th October, in company with Britain, France and Turkey (the first two somewhat unenthusiastic), they invited Egypt to take an honourable place in M.E.D.O. and formally apprised the other members of the Arab League and Israel, all of whom were also asked to join. The upshot was never in doubt. Egypt dryly side-stepped these advances and the entire Arab world expressed total disapproval of the plan.

Thus did the Arabs clearly proclaim the doctrine of Arab neutralism which they had formulated long before. It will always be surprising that the West took so long to appreciate the significance. The one thought of the Arab peoples was to free themselves from foreign rule, by which they meant the various forms of influence exercised by the West. Some of them, such as the Egyptians and Iraqis, were set on putting an end to what remained of British occupation with the result that in these two countries local issues took precedence for some time over the Palestinian situation. But as country after country won complete independence, 'Israeli aggression' became the dominant issue by which all external events were judged. The Arab world became more and more obsessed with the Arab-Israeli conflict, in its eyes the only topic that mattered. The East–West conflict did not interest the Arabs nor would they listen to the free world's anti-Soviet propaganda. Nothing counted with them except the threat from Israel; they refused to regard the U.S.S.R. as in any way an enemy. Soviet domination, which would, they imagined, humour Arab susceptibilities, seemed a lesser catastrophe (should it ever come to pass) than Israeli domination with its inevitable concomitant, the extirpation of panarabism.

Arab statesmen made no attempt to hide these feelings but their words went unheeded in the West. To take a representative example: Maaruf Dawalibi, a one-time student in Paris, had one day in May 1946 exchanged passports on Orly airport with the grand mufti Haj Amin, thus enabling the latter to escape from France undetected. In Syria Dawalibi was first a deputy of the Populist Party, then Minister of Economics and President of the Chamber, and even briefly Prime Minister. The Arabs, he proclaimed to the Arab League in March 1950, 'would a thousand times rather become a Soviet republic than the victims of Israel'. And on hearing of the Western defence proposals he said on 17th October 1951: 'If speed is essential, an end must first be put to the aggression from which the Arab world has actually suffered before we need worry about repelling an aggression which is still remote and uncertain. Israeli aggression is an indisputable fact.

If the alliance now offered us is not to put a stop to Israeli aggression, what interest can it have for us?' At the same time one of his political opponents, Akram Hourani, a socialist and the leader of the Arab Renaissance Party (the Baath), declared on 22nd October, 1951, that the defence plan was no more than 'an imperialist scheme for the partition of the Middle East into spheres of influence. The British and the Americans must choose between the friendship of the Arabs and the friendship of the Jews. The Russians are in any case not our enemies. Our enemies are the imperialist Powers which occupy our countries and support Israel against us.' The Moslem Brotherhood sang the same song; its leader in Syria, Sheikh Mustafa Sebai, declared on 12th May, 1950: 'We shall ally ourselves with Russia, be it the devil.'

Chapter 5

Fresh Western moves in Cairo and Baghdad

The United States and Britain persevered, but quite apart from competition between them for influence in one place or another, they failed to keep in step because they concentrated on different questions and adopted different methods.

The Americans, convinced of the importance of Egypt (even more so after the coup of 1952), wanted to make it the Middle Eastern centre of their defence system and so greatly expand this system in depth. They therefore urged the British to make substantial political concessions to Egypt and withdraw their troops in order to pave the way for reconciliation with the West, but they did not begin to get results until the Anglo-Egyptian treaty was initialled on 27th July and signed on 19th October, 1954. By that treaty the Egyptian government, having secured the evacuation of the canal zone, agreed to allow the bases in the zone to be maintained and guarded and authorized their 're-activation' in the event of war or the threat of war against the Arab countries, and even against Turkey.

The inclusion of Turkey (the British failed to add Iran) was a hardly won concession which seemed so onerous to the Egyptian government that it refused for the time being to acquaint the Egyptian people with the more far-reaching military engagements sought by the Americans.

All the same President Nasser gave the American public some fairly extensive assurances. On 3rd August, 1954, he told the *Associated Press* correspondent that Egypt wanted American aid and even, in the event of aggression, military support and therefore regarded itself as openly at war with Russian-inspired communism and would in future orient its foreign policy rather towards the West than towards the East.

From this point, there was a palpable intensification of the American desire completely to win over the southern Arab states and particularly Egypt. Demonstrations of friendship, sometimes naïve, were multiplied. The leader of a delegation sent to Cairo by the 'American Friends of the Middle East' declared that 'one of the biggest mistakes an American business man could make would be to underestimate the capacity, intelligence, honesty and character of the peoples of the Middle East'. At the request of King Saud a statue of Mahomet was hurriedly removed from the Law Courts in New York and destroyed because it offended against the strict precepts of Islam. At the beginning of 1955 the State Department gave concrete expression to its wish for a rapprochement with Egypt by putting Mr. George Allen in charge of Middle Eastern affairs and sending as Ambassador to Cairo Mr. Henry Byroade, whose every move was made with a view to pleasing President Nasser's government.

But Egypt was not in a position to make many concessions. As M. Marcel Colombe has observed, alluding to the attempt on President Nasser's life on 26th October by a member of the Moslem Brotherhood: 'The eight bullets that whistled past Colonel Abdel Nasser's ears only a few days after the conclusion of the treaty with London had clearly shown where the limits lay.'

Meanwhile, however, the United States had as a side line lavished fairly extensive military aid on other countries of the Middle East. Iraq in particular enjoyed such aid from 21st April, 1954. A military assistance pact was concluded on 10th May, 1954, with Pakistan which was a member of the South East Asia Treaty Organization (SEATO) and linked in a sense with Nato by way of the Turco-Pakistani treaty of 4th April. Furthermore the strategic arming and equipment of Turkey were proceeding apace.

Nevertheless, contrary to a commonly held belief, it was not the Americans who first conceived the idea of an anti-Russian defence organization in the 'northern tier' of the Middle East. This plan is better ascribed to the British who wished to exploit and concert various tendencies in its direction which were current in certain Middle Eastern states. Turkey especially favoured any plan which, by increasing the flow of Western aid, would reinforce it against its traditional Russian enemy and against communism, increase its economic strength and at the same time add to its political influence in the Arab world. Iraq wanted to escape from dependence on a single Western Power and become associated instead with the West as a whole; it was also keen to receive arms in order to increase its standing in the Middle East and its claim to that leadership of the Arabs of which, in bitter competition with Egypt, it never ceased to dream.

In this set of circumstances Britain spied a way of achieving something which it had almost given up in despair – a new contractual basis for British relations with Iraq in place of the old relationship which had been sapped by the passage of time and the general turn of events. The Anglo-Iraqi treaty, which had been very much ahead of the times in 1930, had begun to date within ten years. Baghdad could hardly be expected to put up with unequal treaties and the occupation of bases by the British after Damascus and Beirut had got rid of the French and could boast of complete independence.

The British government realized this. A new and more liberal treaty was concluded at Portsmouth in 1948 but it was still too unequal for national sentiment in Iraq, and Baghdad refused to ratify it. But the British were well aware of the urgent need to replace the treaty of 1930 which was due to expire in 1957, and they came to the conclusion that the easiest way of doing this was to insert themselves into a wider military alliance (including Iraq) within which they would be able easily and inconspicuously to make special arrangements with Iraq. In this way Britain would succeed in giving its political relations with Iraq a new lease of life, in giving this old Hashemite ally a better handicap in the Arab stakes, in becoming a Western partner in a Middle Eastern defence organization, and in restoring its credit and influence in the Middle East.

This policy won a cool reception in the United States, since it cut across the wish of the Americans as far as possible to step into the shoes of an apparently played-out Britain; but it fitted in with the Americans' major preoccupation – to build breakwaters against the U.S.S.R. – and so Washington backed it in spite of its imperfections.

Such were the motives and manœuvres which led to the Baghdad Pact. They were patently circumscribed and it is astounding that a venture which was destined substantially to commit the whole West and to change the balance of the Arab world should have been conducted with so little serious consideration and no inkling of its probable long term consequences.

A Turco-Iraqi pact of mutual assistance was signed at Baghdad on 24th February, 1955, after several months occupied by limited agreements, extensive conversations and persistent press reports (sometimes in very nervous tones, as in Lebanon). This pact, to which other states might adhere, was to become known as the 'Baghdad Pact'. After referring to the Turco-Iraqi treaty of 29th March, 1946, the signatories declared that, as members of the United Nations, they bore 'great responsibilities . . . concerned with the maintenance of peace and security in the Middle East'; they noted that the Arab League joint defence treaty could not, by its terms, affect the rights and obligations accruing from the United Nations charter and they therefore resolved to co-operate in accordance with article 51 of that charter with the object of safeguarding their security and defence (article 1). They affirmed that the pact ran counter to none of their international obligations (article 4); they provided that 'the pact shall be open for accession to any member of the Arab League or any other State actively concerned with the security and peace in this region' (article 5) and declared that 'when at least four Powers become parties to the pact, a permanent Council at ministerial level will be set up' (article 6).

No other Arab country joined the pact but Pakistan adhered to it on September 23rd and Iran on October 25th, the latter after much hesitation and after being at pains to conciliate the U.S.S.R. by emphasizing that the pact was purely defensive.

Great Britain became a party to it on April 5th and concluded a special defence agreement with Iraq within its framework. By this agreement Britain assumed the responsibility for the pact's Western connections and a privileged position in giving military aid and advice to Iraq; Britain undertook to go to Iraq's assistance on demand and if necessary to make armed forces available if Iraq were attacked or threatened with attack. Britain abandoned its bases in Iraq but retained transit facilities which, together with British training missions and maintenance tasks, preserved for Britain a significant military status in Iraq. At the time of the revolution of 14th July, 1958, Britain turned out to have no fewer than 2,200 nationals at Habbaniya.

The pact was ill received in the Arab world. Cairo considered, quite rightly, that it was directed against Egypt on more counts than one and tried to form a coalition of the other Arab states against Iraq within the Arab League. But the statutes of the League required decisions to be unanimous with the result that Iraq had no difficulty in defeating Egypt's move, but the League itself was plunged on the eve of its tenth anniversary into a crisis which weakened it for a long time to come and was even accounted by some a mortal blow.

Defeated, disillusioned and convinced that they had been tricked by the Anglo-Saxons the Egyptians meditated other courses. 'From that moment,' says M. Marcel Colombe, 'the Russo-Egyptian rapprochement was bound to follow. It was an ineluctable and, what is more, predictable result of the Baghdad Pact and Iraqi-Egyptian hostility. For Egypt there was no escaping it – the more so since the Bandung conference of 1955 showed President Nasser how much there was to be gained by a neutralist policy in his contest with Iraq. Neutralism was put to service in the cause of Egyptian nationalism and the U.S.S.R. was the first to benefit.'

Syria and Lebanon were hardly less hostile to the new pact. In Syria the parliamentary régime, recently restored, was functioning uneasily to the tune of a multiplication of unstable parties, and the stock of the Left was rising. Lebanon was enjoying a peaceful period but the delicate balance between its commitments was, as ever, susceptible to outside upheavals. These two states had good reason to fear for their independence if Iraq's ambitions were to become more categoric and its forces stronger. Turkey moreover made a tactless attempt to apply pressure on them which was very ill received. France on the other hand showed a proper understanding of the forces at work and did not conceal its distaste for the pact. Invoking the tripartite declaration of 1950 Paris recalled that it was opposed, as all the signatories of that declaration should be, to any changes of frontiers in the Middle East; it thus lent discreet support to Syrian and Lebanese opposition to any 'Fertile Crescent' scheme.

But what was done could not be undone. No amount of objection could deflect the protagonists of the pact, who were sure that they had discovered a practicable way of organizing the defence of the Middle East and sidestepping the Palestine problem. Even the Americans, overcoming their initial coolness, decided that it was 'realistic' to show interest in the pact 'since it existed' and, without formally acceding to it, provided significant and valuable support which amounted in effect to open patronage.

But it was foolish to imagine that Arab-Israeli hostility could be sidestepped and ignored. The attempt to by-pass this dilemma involved falling into another which became even more fateful. It was a cardinal error to imagine that the U.S.S.R. would sit back and allow a 'northern tier' to be consolidated as an element in the policy of containment without doing anything about it.

PART V

THE PERIOD OF SOVIET INTERVENTION (1955 AND AFTER)

Chapter 1

The Russians appear on the scene

THE RELATIONS OF the U.S.S.R. with Islam and the peoples of Asia have seldom been correctly interpreted in the West. In particular, modern Russia's attitude towards the Arab part of the Middle East has usually been considered from too narrow an angle. Too much attention has been focused on minor matters, moves of limited significance and personal incidents as though the observers were policemen carrying out an investigation and unmasking a plot, and the conclusions drawn from this procedure have been too hasty and too general to have any real value.

Particularly since 1945, if an Orthodox prelate went to Moscow, or a Russian trade mission visited Yemen, or the staff of the Russian embassy in Cairo was increased, or Tiflis radio changed its programmes, or a communist cell was discovered in Baghdad, or a fellow-travelling club was formed in Beirut, or a communist was elected to parliament in Damascus, the Western press triumphantly pinpointed a manœuvre by the Kremlin.

What is more, in Western eyes Russian policy seemed weak and full of mistakes. The Russians did not dare to persist in their pressure on Turkey, allowed northern Iran to slip from their grasp, and made no move in favour of local communists when these were arrested. They were vacillating and ambivalent with regard to Israel and could not, so it was believed, get on really good terms with practising Moslems. In fact, they were only conducting obscure sapping operations, appealing to the discontented and the perplexed, winning a few adherents, and flirting with governments (such as the Egyptian) whose relations with the West were strained.

Therefore all the West needed to do was to support reactionary governments which were taking steps to combat Soviet propaganda, and if possible increase their number or at least their efficiency. It was all a question of vigilance.

But what usually escaped Western notice was the fact that Soviet overt actions in the Middle East were no more than relatively unimportant opening gambits. Over and above these sallies it ought not to have been difficult to detect that there were tactical and strategic plans afoot and that it was nonsense to expect the U.S.S.R. to rest content with a policy of pinpricks. Moscow's gambit was, in fact, the simplest of all gambits: to exploit the mistakes of its adversary.

In particular the Russians were exploiting the albatross of the West – its impotence in the face of the Arab-Israeli conflict and its plain inability to appreciate the importance (indeed the total pre-eminence) of the Palestine grievance. The Russians knew that the West was, in this, bound to disappoint and exasperate the Arabs, who would then turn to the U.S.S.R. Nor, from the Russian point of view, was it even necessary that the Arabs should openly take Moscow's side; it would be enough for them to desert Washington and London. Their neutrality was alone enough to foil Western plans since the West aimed at active Arab participation in the defence of the free world. The Arabs' obsession with their conflict with Israel inevitably led them to treat the contest between the two world blocks as null and void. Such was Arab nationalism, open and avowed from 1950 onwards.

Thenceforward the chips were down. All Moscow had to do was wait and watch; Western misinterpretations of the Arab Middle East added to the confusion in the area nearly every time the West took action. A favourable opportunity was bound to occur. The Baghdad Pact gave the Russians their opportunity and they seized it the more swiftly because that inept diplomatic instrument constituted a military threat of a kind to themselves.

Perhaps a fable in the eastern manner may here be introduced. The Russians in the Middle East were like a poacher who is kept under observation because he occasionally snares a little game but is too canny to get caught by the keeper or the owner. One fine day they think they have found a way of catching him. So they go to settle his score but lo! he has seduced the daughter of the house who, with an absurd excess of caution, has never been allowed out into the town. In despair she has thrown herself at the fellow's head, thinking at one and the same time to get her own back and to emancipate herself, while also assuring herself that she will know how to get rid of the fellow once she is satisfied and 'free'.

The West held the Arab nation on a leash and sought to ignore its restlessness. So the Arab nation gave itself to the Russians who had noted its desires and promised to assuage them.

There is a story, perhaps apocryphal, which pinpoints an evening in the autumn of 1955 as the opening of the new phase in Middle Eastern affairs which was marked by definite Russian intervention. President Nasser was talking to the Russian military attaché at a reception in Cairo. Half seriously, half jokingly, perhaps merely by way of small talk, perhaps to sound out the ground, he asked the Russian officer if by any chance the U.S.S.R. could sell him arms. The Russian bowed solemnly and said he would enquire. Forty-eight hours later the Russian ambassador asked for an audience and said that the answer was yes.

This one word found the West's Achilles heel. The Baghdad Pact, if read in conjunction with the tripartite declaration of 1950, made plain the fact that the Arab Middle East was to receive arms for an East-West war which was no concern of the Arabs, and that they were forbidden to use these arms in the Arab-Israeli conflict on their doorstep. This Western policy amounted not merely to a naïve neglect of Arab sentiment; it also tended to perpetuate in the Middle East just the kind of indirect influence that most irked local opinion. After political 'mandates' over governments and then economic 'mandates' over resources, the West had produced a sort of military 'mandate' over arms. Even if the word itself was never used, that was how it seemed in local eyes.

The delivery of Eastern arms without strings, triumphantly announced on 27th September, 1955, enabled Egypt and then the other Arab countries to discard the last vestiges of subjection to the West and at last to feel perfectly free. By the same token sentence was passed on the frail armistice between Israel and the Arab states without the possibility of reprieve, for thenceforward the least incident would call in question the *status quo* which the West had been trying to erect into a charter for the Middle East ever since 1950. The tragedy of the autumn of 1956 began to take shape. The U.S.S.R. rocked the Middle East – not, as people had liked to think, by long and laborious intrigues (some of which were real enough) but by a single stroke of astounding political genius.

It was a dramatic coup. Although the Russian offer took the world by surprise, it fitted into the political and social trends in the Middle East like a hand into a glove.

The chief features of this development have already been outlined. Its principal characteristics were not the classic rise of local communist parties nor the growth of diplomatic and commercial relations with governments, nor direct propaganda. The scene was dominated by two basic developments of the preceding years – the Arab-Israeli contest which gave rise to Arab neutralism and caused the Arabs to adopt in external affairs an attitude wholly favourable to Russian policy and strategy, and secondly, the rise of a popular and unifying nationalism (*qawmiya*) which gradually overlaid national patriotism (*wataniya*), vowed social movements to the service of Arab unity and promoted attitudes of mind conducive to an extreme left wing mystique.

If it was to make an effective reply to the Soviet challenge, the West – and particularly the Americans – needed to understand the nature and origins of what had come to pass. Failing such understanding, any attempt to change their policy was unlikely; they were bound to give it new adjuncts and impetus without changing its direction.

The members of the Baghdad Pact and its unofficial associates, the United States, were caught by a political parachute drop in the rear of the pact and their first riposte was to strengthen the pact's resources and multiply its functions. They hoped, it seemed, to make it something more than a safety catch against external aggression and to use it to prevent internal disorders, strengthen its members generally, and attract neighbouring countries which might be tempted by other possibilities.

At the first plenary meeting of the pact, on 21st and 22nd November, 1955, the members explicitly adopted as their objective the suppression of subversion within their borders and established an 'anti-subversion committee' which the United States joined without joining the pact itself.

In the spring of 1956 Iran invoked the pact in order to obtain Iraqi co-operation against the Jawanrudi tribe which was thus deprived of its usual expedient of taking refuge beyond the frontier; the perennial disturbance of this small Kurdish tribe was ascribed without much justification to communist influence. At a further meeting in June and July 1956 the committee expressed anxiety about the increased versatility of subversive activities in the area and urged prompt and effective counter-measures. Under the same head, Turkey raised the question of communist activities in Syria in November 1956.

At their first session the members of the pact also set themselves constructive tasks designed to increase the well-being and prosperity of the peoples of the area. An economic committee, which like the anti-subversion committee was soon strengthened by American membership, came into existence in the spring of 1956. The British representative on the pact, who was a member of this committee, stressed the urgency of economic projects within the framework of the pact to which he had no difficulty in getting his Middle Eastern colleagues to agree. A beginning was made with schemes of various kinds – common planning of hydro-electric resources on either side of frontiers, a railway from Ankara to Teheran and Karachi, air transport agreements, a telecommunication system, and even improvement in cattle breeding and the co-ordination of veterinary services.

Washington's primary concern with strategic equipment seemed to be offset by London's apparent intention to recreate a fountain-head of economic influence, if not economic control, on the lines of the wartime Middle East Supply Centre. But the economic and financial advantages of membership of the pact, substantial though they were, could never be sufficiently so to induce other states to join. In order to achieve this result, the Americans would have had to concentrate their economic and technical aid exclusively on the pact members, but this they could not contemplate since they remained intent on winning all the Middle East, and especially Egypt, to their side.

The pact therefore proved disappointing; it barely impinged upon the seductive potentialities of Russian aid. These were considerable, based as they were on the U.S.S.R.'s own direct experience at home of under-development and speedy remedies for it; on the U.S.S.R.'s ability to remind the Middle East, with a mixture of coyness and shrewdness, that the Russians had themselves been in the same position a generation before; and on the U.S.S.R.'s success in making itself a first class Power, politically and economically, in a single generation. The Middle East had only to follow the approved methods, the rules and regulations for which would be imparted by the Russians together with practical aid in applying them.

Moreover the methods were comparatively simple and, unlike those of the capitalist West, in no way departed from the principle of the equality of sovereign states; they were therefore as well adapted to Russian opportunities as to Middle Eastern needs. The Russians would supply industrial equipment which, by its very simplicity, was well suited to the needs of a developing country and which they could easily make available (with the help, if need be, of satellites like Czechoslovakia or Poland) since they themselves were concentrating at home on heavy industry and consumer goods. In exchange the Middle Eastern countries would deliver primary products (including their chancy surpluses of cotton and cereals), much needed in the U.S.S.R. where agriculture had fallen victim to the collectivist mystique and a huge population was waiting to absorb them.

Thus was forged a simple and practical series of exchanges well calculated to seduce the mind and heart and to satisfy elementary needs. At the end of 1955 Egypt subscribed and a few months later the attractions completely overwhelmed Syria.

Although Russian aid was so well suited to the circumstances and so ably proffered, the West was not so lacking in inspiration as to be incapable of a reply from the vast armoury of its industrial and financial riches. But unfortunately it was not so masterly as the Russians. Western, or more precisely American, retaliation was hampered by capitalist complications and hidebound methods, and by the interplay of politicians and administrators who lacked a compelling common motive; finally by a divided and extraordinarily changeable public opinion which frequently overrode the careful calculations of officialdom. In addition, the American riposte was rooted in a political doctrine which was insensitive to the psychology of foreign peoples, reluctant to learn by current experience, and inspired to the point of absurdity by grandiose and quasi-mystical notions; it prided itself, for instance, on its practical approach while in fact dealing with the frightening hazards of the 'calculated risk'.

It must in fairness be added that the Middle Eastern members of the partnership, convinced that they could always raise the stakes, made no allowances for the domestic difficulties and other limitations that beset their Western partners, whom they made no attempt to consider or to enlighten. The elements of misunderstanding were all too present.

Chapter 2

The West hesitates at Aswan and splits at Suez

The test came over the Aswan high dam in the winter of 1955–56 and the following spring. The topic was apposite, for the dam was vital to Egypt; the stake was immense, because this was the issue on which, if any, it might be possible to swing the Middle East. And the instrument was to hand, because the undertaking, for all its vastness, was by no means beyond the financial and technical resources of the West but could knock out the U.S.S.R. On the very morrow of a dangerous Russian challenge, providence offered a chance to show the Middle East once and for all in which quarter its interests really lay. But through clumsiness this unique opportunity was lamentably lost.

The plan for a high dam at Aswan was nothing more nor less than a matter of life and death for Egypt, whose population was increasing by leaps and bounds while its resources were static. Given its existing irrigation system Egypt was tilling all the land that could be tilled, and agricultural reform – which, if it ever materialized, would rectify social injustices – would in the short run diminish rather than increase already inadequate agricultural yields. On the other hand the proposed high dam at Aswan would give Egypt the use of the whole of its share of the Nile waters by storing the seasonal flood; an additional 850,000 hectares would be cultivable, drainage would be much more efficient, and the river would be navigable from one end of Egypt to the other. Finally, it would provide ten million kilowatt-hours of low cost electricity and thereby multiply thirtyfold the industrial potentialities of the Nile valley.

The work, which was to take ten years, was estimated to cost $1,400 million, of which at least $400 million would be needed in hard currency. The International Bank for Reconstruction and Development (the World Bank) decided that the scheme was feasible and agreed to co-operate on its usual terms, i.e., interest on its loans at $3\frac{1}{2}\%$, repayment of the capital in twenty years, technical control of the project, supervision of the borrower's national budget and a veto on the borrower's further contracts, and a guaranteed and substantial financial contribution by at least one other state. On these conditions the Bank was willing to advance $200 million. The United States and Britain were ready to put up $56 million and $14 million respectively and ultimately to find the remainder of the foreign currency required ($130 million).

But at this point the U.S.S.R. let it be known it was ready to provide aid on more favourable and liberal terms and the Egyptians thought themselves adroit enough to escape the financial and economic controls which the Western lenders required by playing one side off against the other. At the least, Cairo hoped for some open recognition that the transaction was not a service rendered by the Anglo-Saxons but a prize won by them, and made plain its expectation of enticing offers from Eastern countries and private concerns.

During the winter of 1955–56 an anti-Egyptian current set in in certain Anglo-Saxon circles. London began to be worried about the interests of the other riparian states, especially of the Sudan which had won its independence and escaped Egyptian influence and now saw a piece of its territory scheduled for inundation under the plan. London felt that a general agreement on the division of the Nile waters ought to precede the conclusion of a financial agreement with Egypt.

Washington's misgivings were more complicated. American Jewry, overlooking the advantages of deflecting Egyptian chauvinism from the vision of revenge against Israel to constructive activities in the south, complained that aid to Israel was being subordinated to aid to Egypt. The southern Democrats, with their special concern for the cotton growers of their states, looked askance at an undertaking which seemed to deal trumps to their Egyptian competitors, and the Right was indignant with Egypt's reluctance to join the fight against communism and with Cairo's firm commitments to Moscow. There was moreover a more general factor at work in Congress, which was growing allergic to the whole American foreign aid programme and was planning both to diminish the total sum and to attach more stringent conditions by insisting that eighty per cent. of any future allocation should take the form of loans and not grants. In the case of the Aswan dam any such new condition would affect the attitude of the World Bank which was nervous that Egypt's economy and finances would be crippled by an over-load of annual interest payments. All these factors helped to add up to a reminder to the authorities in Washington that a presidential election was in the offing.

Meanwhile Egypt, so far from trying to arrest the deterioration in the climate of American opinion, added new grounds for discontent by recognizing the Chinese government in Peking and pressing on with negotiations for Russian aid. At the same time Cairo forgot that there was a time limit to its manœuvres since by American rules the American offer had to be accepted before June 30th, the end of the fiscal year.

At the beginning of July 1956 the American offer was cancelled from the formal book-keeping point of view, but Washington simultaneously announced that there was no change in American policy towards Egypt and that a fresh allocation remained possible. There was no reaction from President Nasser for several days. From Jugoslavia, where Marshal Tito may have dispelled some of his illusions about the workings of the Soviet mind, he telegraphed to his ambassador in Washington to accept whatever the cost. But when Egypt's representative was received at the State Department on July 19th, the verdict handed out to him was a categoric refusal, and a few days later the offers made by Britain and the World Bank were likewise withdrawn. Almost at the same moment, it became clear that there was to be no immediate Soviet aid for the high dam, although the Russians repeated their willingness to help Egyptian industrial development.

Mr. Dulles' decision was welcomed with something not far short of enthusiasm in the British, French and American press. To judge by Western newspapers Nasser had suffered a severe setback, his blackmailing policy had been condemned to failure by a display of strength and the virtues of clear-headedness and his adventurous ways had landed him between two stools. A calculated risk had been taken; Moscow was bound to assume obligations on which it could but default, with the result that a disillusioned and wiser Egypt would turn back to the West. The *New York Herald-Tribune* was almost unique in keeping its head, advising the State Department to try to bring the Egyptian President's power into the right proportions, since when one makes an enemy one must treat him as such. More typical was Mr. Dulles' attitude eight months later when the consequences of the American withdrawal were plain for all to see; while denying that he had had any intention of engaging in a trial of strength with the Russians, he calmly enumerated his motives as if they were wholly valid. To cite the *New York Herald-Tribune* once more (Mr. Stewart Alsop's column) the Secretary of State must have been impelled by an overriding wish to please certain groups at home when he claimed as heroic this bold move designed to show up the hollowness of Russian offers.

The details of this Aswan business are worth study because there is no better example of the West's fundamental incompetence in its dealings with a Middle East galvanized by the prospect of Russian aid. Nasser, we know, felt the American withdrawal to be a slap in the face and reacted by nationalizing the Suez canal. This event and its consequences have been the subject of so much analysis and comment that there is no need to dwell on them at any length.

The nationalization of the canal was not difficult to foretell. However skilful the Company's management and however wise its policies (which expressly eschewed 'playing politics'), it could hardly hope to escape the fate of all those major undertakings in the Middle East which were suspected of being means to indirect Western domination. Admittedly, some argued that Egypt would gain nothing by an early take-over of a concern which entailed complicated techniques and which would in any case revert to it upon the expiry of the concession in 1968. Others held that once the British garrisons had been removed from the canal zone, Egypt would be eager to complete the emancipation of Egyptian territory by expropriating the Company.[1] To all appearances Nasser had nationalization in mind but as a more or less remote project. Suddenly, on July 26th, 1956, he took the plunge for a number of reasons of varying importance.

The first and most instinctive was his determination not to take a humiliating rebuff lying down. His action was a bold retort which gave him the last word. The second and official reason was the appropriation of canal dues for the building of the high dam, but the logic of this argument was much open to question. The most powerful reason was the one which Nasser may well not have perceived at the time – the fact that the nationalization of the canal would set the Western Powers by the ears.

The Americans, the volume of whose traffic through the canal was small and whose financial stake in the operating Company was nil, were not much affected by its nationalization. With the British and French things were the other way about; they were deeply involved and their wrath was understandable quite apart from its apparently strong justification in law. It led them, after various fruitless attempts to produce an international settlement, to embark on direct action of which the consequences were both foreseeable and (especially for themselves) disastrous. It is melancholy to reflect that the long record of Anglo-French hostility in the Middle East was finally brought to a close by agreement on so ill conceived an adventure.

During that summer of 1956, too many people were occupied in counting the blessings to be expected from a forceful dis-

[1] A prophetic but unnoticed article by a French journalist in Cairo, F. Courtal, made this point in the Lebanese paper *Orient* on July 15th, 1956 ('Will the British evacuation of the Suez canal mean the retreat of the Company as well?'). The article was dated June 22nd.

lodgement of Nasser rather than calculating the chances of successful completion of any operation against him. At least two adverse factors were discernible. First, the operation could not be confined to Egypt because it would inevitably provoke displays of Arab solidarity for which provision needed to be made – in particular by guarding the pipe lines between Iraq and the Mediterranean. Secondly, and even more important, the U.S.S.R. was already too deeply involved in Middle Eastern affairs to let pass an adventure which would humiliate its customers and establish a Western political and strategic stronghold on the glacis of the neutralist Arab world. London and Paris rushed upon their fate because they had misinterpreted the force of Arab nationalism and the extent of Russian penetration in the Middle East, because in a word they had failed to gauge the nature of the current Eastern Question.

Admittedly Arab solidarity did not at first operate entirely in Egypt's favour. The Iraqi government, while endorsing the legal right to nationalize the canal, reaffirmed its loyalty to the Baghdad Pact and carefully refrained from open criticism of British policy. The Lebanese government was extremely non-committal. But every other Arab cabinet supported Cairo and popular opinion was avid for resistance, scenting the chance given to Nasser to refurbish his prestige. The Egyptian dictator was not slow to exploit this sudden fillip to his popularity and he was able to bring decisive influence to bear on the elections in progress in Jordan; King Hussein did not dare to summon Iraqi troops to give support to the moderates, with the result that an almost wholly pro-Egyptian parliament was elected on October 21st, 1956. The new cabinet in Amman immediately adhered to the Syrian-Egyptian defence pact of October 20th, 1955 (which had been supplemented by a convention with Saudi Arabia on October 27th and a defence pact between Egypt, Yemen and Saudi Arabia on April 21st, 1956). Thus two days after the Jordanian elections a close Egyptian-Syrian-Jordanian military coalition had been formed under the Egyptian General Hakim Amr, who became commander-in-chief of the forces of all three countries and set off without delay on a tour of inspection of Amman and Damascus.

Israel, which had not unreasonably been seriously alarmed by the provision of Russian arms to Arab countries, regarded the new Arab military coalition, which almost completely encircled it, as a grave threat to its existence and decided to take action before the unified Arab command could organize itself and the Egyptian troops and their allies learn the use of their new and modern weapons. A preventive campaign seemed the least of various evils. In the night of October 29th–30th, Israeli forces crossed the demarcation line, invaded Sinai and completely routed the Egyptians in a matter of hours.

There followed a whole series of interventions of evil memory. On October 30th the British and French called on the combatants to separate. On the 31st they took matters into their own hands and began to bombard Egyptian airfields. The Egyptians 'sabotaged' the canal by sinking a number of vessels, and military and civilian groups blew up the Iraq Petroleum Company's pipe line in Syria.

On November 6th the British and the French, having taken Port Said, were forced to suspend operations at the bidding of the United Nations which decided to despatch an international force. The attitude of the United States and the U.S.S.R. had saved Egypt from a complete and crushing military defeat. Britain, however, told the Eastern members of the Baghdad Pact that their representations had been a strong contributory factor in the decision to break off operations.

It was soon clear that the balance sheet of the crisis was very different from anything the protagonists had expected. Everything was topsy-turvy. The British and the French had meant to bring Nasser down but he had survived their attack, had in turn struck a serious economic blow at their oil supplies, and had won a clear diplomatic victory which was soon turned into a military victory by a propaganda machine admirably attuned to Arab flights of imagination and emotion. His standing in the

Middle East was therefore enormously and unexpectedly enhanced.

This Egyptian triumph was shared by other Arabs notwithstanding the fact that none of them had made the slightest move to engage the Israelis on their demarcation lines. Syria had seized the opportunity to cut the pipe line (a double-barrelled achievement which deprived the West of oil and Iraq of royalties) and also to destroy the French cruiser *Jean Bart* which was torpedoed off Port Said (as everybody in the Middle East was soon told) by a patrolling frigate commanded by a Christian from Aleppo. This exploit was commemorated on Egyptian postage stamps, and streets in most Arab towns were renamed after the hero, Jules Jamal.

The United Nations came well out of the crisis, not so much for securing a cease-fire (which was clearly due to the pressure exerted by the two major Powers) or for its work in putting the canal into service again, as for the work of its international force. By separating the Israelis and Arabs on the southern demarcation line and by holding the entrance to the Gulf of Akaba at Sharm es Sheikh, this force 'froze' the Israeli-Egyptian conflict (though temperatures remained high on the Jordan border) and mitigated the stranglehold on Israel by opening a passage to the Red Sea.

Judged on a basis of hard fact, Russian aid to Cairo looked meagre. Russian arms had not brought the Arabs victory, and had in fact been of less use to the Egyptians in Sinai than they would be henceforth to the Israelis who captured them in great quantities, sometimes intact in their packing cases. There was some rejoicing over the fact that the Russian game had been shown up and Western eyes opened, albeit a year late. This, said M. Guy Mollet on November 12th, was the positive result of an operation which he unblushingly refused to regret or disavow. Again, it could be plausibly argued that the Russian threat uttered to Britain and France had had no practical effect, since the two Powers would in any case have complied with the decision of the United Nations.

But none of these praiseworthy reflections held good outside the Western world. Among Arabs Russian prestige was greatly increased by Moscow's attitude during the Suez crisis. No other Great Power had proffered complete, spontaneous and effective friendship and support. Russian sincerity and disinterest had been put to the test and in Arab eyes had been proved beyond question or cavil. Consequently Arab expectations rose higher than ever and embraced not only economic and technical aid on the least irksome and onerous conditions but also massive and virtually unconditional diplomatic support.

Chapter 3

The Americans intervene

In all this there was more emotion than logic. The Americans discovered, to their naïve surprise, that their severity towards Britain and France evoked no gratitude whatever from the Arabs. If they expected to win Arab favour by their attitude, their plans miscarried. Mr. Adlai Stevenson, the unsuccessful Democratic candidate for the Presidency, was clear sighted enough to deplore (on November 1st) a policy which brought the United States into the same camp at the United Nations with the U.S.S.R. and the Egyptian dictator against the British, French and Israeli democracies. He concluded that never in the course of history had American diplomacy suffered a set-back so serious, complete and catastrophic. But the administration in Washington expressed on December 3rd the hope that the United States would be able to 'assist in bringing about a permanent settlement of the other persistent conflicts which had plagued the Middle East over recent years'.

Under cover of this modest formula Washington set out to propound a 'new deal' and to fill the dangerous 'power vacuum' created by the elimination of Britain and France from the Middle East. This phrase was not relished except on the far side of the Atlantic. London and Paris were unnecessarily offended, since even those most opposed to the Suez operation were unwilling to believe that the achievements and connections of centuries could, or deserved to be, wiped out by what they regarded as an aberration. The Arab pride of Cairo and Damascus was ruffled. What is more the word vacuum was inapposite. In fact the Middle Eastern forum was filled with the resounding play and counterplay of Arab emotions inexpertly directed offstage by the Russian producer and prompter. This unfortunate theory of the 'vacuum', which was taken up by the American press, destroyed in advance the psychological advantages America hoped to reap from its next proposals.

President Eisenhower first conferred with Mr. Hammarskjöld (the tidying-up after the crisis being in the hands of the United Nations) and then on December 31st announced the broad lines of his plan for the development of the Middle East. The United States would oppose, if necessary by force, any Russian aggression in the area and would devote $400–500 million over two years to a massive aid programme designed to stop political infiltration and subversion by strengthening anti-communist elements in the several countries.

Such was the Eisenhower Doctrine. It came into force at once, although it was not published in final form until March 9th, 1957, after the conclusion of the necessary constitutional formalities. In the interests of speed the President of the United States was authorized to co-operate and assist any nation or group of nations in the general area of the Middle East in the development of economic strength dedicated to the maintenance of national independence. He might negotiate military aid programmes with any nation that so desired, in include 'the employment of the armed forces of the United States' to help any nation or group of nations which sought such assistance 'against overt armed aggression from any nation controlled by international communism.' Finally, during the current fiscal year the President might allocate authorized credits up to $200 million for the economic and military purposes envisaged.

The Russians were not slow to reply. On February 11th Mr. Shepilov suggested a Western 'quadripartite declaration' on the Middle East, thus inaugurating the new look of Russian diplomacy. The three Western chancelleries merely declined the suggestion, in the not unreasonable belief that to adopt it would be to give legal recognition to the fact of Russian intervention in Middle Eastern affairs; yet the Western Powers were unable to put forward any positive counter-proposal. The British felt bound to insist on the effective services to peace rendered by the

Baghdad Pact, of which they were members, whereupon President Nasser smartly returned this inept volley and vaunted 'positive neutralism' as against both the Eisenhower Doctrine and the Shepilov plan; he added however that there was a difference between the Russians, who had aided and continued to aid Egypt, and the Americans, who had not.

Over and above its ill judged presentation and a diplomatic fusillade which brought manifest advantage to the Russians and Egyptians, there was a further blow in store for the Eisenhower Doctrine. It began by scoring some illusory successes which disguised its marked defects and encouraged the Americans to pursue it in spite of all criticism and to ridiculous lengths.

The first and most paradoxical of these will o' the wisps was the support, not to say sponsorship, accorded to the great American democracy by the reactionary and mediaeval kingdom of Saudi Arabia. Washington's odd choice was not wholly unjustified. The Americans wanted to give Nasser to understand that they had saved him in spite of themselves and would keep him isolated until he was prepared to subscribe to a general reconciliation. Since they neither could nor would turn to Baghdad, which had refused to break off relations with Britain during the Suez crisis and still showed every inclination to put Britain first, there remained only one possible champion, King Saud; in the eyes of the State Department he was in any event a worthy ally in view of the spiritual, geographical and economic importance of his country. The king was invited to the United States and received with extraordinary courtesies. He was flattered and not unaware of the material advantages to be derived from the part he was being asked to play; and he concluded that with American backing he would be all the better placed to exercise his customary influence in Arab states, while preserving enough room for manœuvre to detach himself at the right moment. He thus became the Middle Eastern advocate of the Eisenhower Doctrine.

An American mission led by Mr. James Richards visited several Middle Eastern countries between March 12th and May

7th. It collected a number of formal adherences (Lebanon, Turkey, Iran, Iraq, etc.) and even the assent of some states, such as Jordan, which did not feel they could adhere formally. The pro-Nasser government in Amman had rejected the 'vacuum' theory at the beginning of January but King Hussein forced the Nabulsi cabinet to resign on April 10th, foiled a plot against himself, and after a courageous fight against military and civilian pro-Nasser groups installed a moderate and loyal government. During this serious crisis, which continued into early May, the young king was strongly backed by Saudi forces and, even more important, by news of the American Sixth Fleet cruising off Beirut. At the time this demonstration looked decisive, though a few months later some British observers took the line that King Hussein had never been in need of this moral support in order to come out on top.

However that might be, the Americans believed that they had discovered an infallible way of settling Middle Eastern affairs. The disillusioning process began in Syria. The backcloth of the Syrian political scene consisted of political assassinations and sentences for conspiracy implicating members of the P.P.S. (the Popular Party of Syria, partisans of a Greater Syria and fascist in its origins), 'moderates' and 'American agents'. In the forefront of the stage were left wing politicians – in particular Baath socialists – and a few soldiers like Colonel Serraj who were bitterly opposed to the landed class in power. Anti-Americanism was intensified in the spring by the Sixth Fleet's demonstrations on behalf of King Hussein and by the American decision to join the military committee of the Baghdad Pact on March 23rd. Salah ed-Din Bitar, the socialist Foreign Minister, decided unhesitatingly that 'the Eisenhower Doctrine and the Baghdad Pact were one and the same thing'.

To replace politicians who had been condemned to death (but later reprieved) bye-elections were due, notably in Damascus, and were fixed for May 4th and 5th. One of the candidates of the 'conservative front' – an opposition rally of pro-Iraqi populists – was the leader of the Moslem Brotherhood, Sheikh

Mustafa Sebai. He was beaten by a left wing coalition that included the communists. The unconcealed sympathy, not to say encouragement, given to him by the Americans merely transformed his personal defeat into a rebuff for Western intervention in alliance with the forces of reaction.

In these circumstances there was nothing surprising about the growth of Syria's feeling of isolation which reached obsessional dimensions during the summer. Syria became convinced that it was being strangled between the Baghdad Pact Powers, Iraq and Turkey, on the one hand and Washington's vassals, Lebanon and Jordan, on the other, and turned after some initial hesitation to the only discernible saviour, the U.S.S.R. To Moscow went Khaled al-Azm, a patrician and a plutocrat who had been induced by political failure to look to the extreme left for a secure base and a fresh start. On August 6th he secured significant amounts of technical and economic aid, soon matched by a generous measure of military aid. Thereupon Damascus announced the discovery of a new plot involving members of the American embassy and reported the matter to the Security Council.

The Department of State despatched ambassador Loy Henderson, who had acquired a reputation for talking the same language as Middle Eastern nationalists after his contribution to the settlement of the difficult Iranian oil dispute. Unfortunately, instead of approaching Damascus direct, he began by making inquiries in Ankara where he met the Iraqi king and regent, and from there went on to Beirut and then back to Washington, announcing that the situation was exceedingly grave. Because the American-Lebanese communiqué of March 16th had linked the Beirut government too closely to the Eisenhower Doctrine, Lebanon could no longer play its traditional mediatory role in the Middle East.

Syria was further stirred by Turkish manœuvres. With the maximum of clamour the government in Damascus ordered what amounted to nation-wide mobilization and the whole population flung itself into the work of digging trenches. On

October 13th Egyptian troops disembarked at Lattakia and were received with delirious acclaim. Even Iraq, making believe that Syria's fears were occasioned by Israel, promised help in the defence of Syrian territory and rejected a Western plan for a pipe line to carry Iraqi oil through Turkey.

At the end of October King Saud offered to mediate between Turkey and Syria but he did not seem to expect his offer to be taken seriously. Damascus declined and the Saudis did not insist. At the beginning of the next month Turco-Syrian tension abated of its own accord; complaints dissolved into thin air. By the end of the Syrian crisis there was only one casualty – the United States, whose incapacity had been exposed for all to see.

Chapter 4

Nasser reshapes panarabism

Arab solidarity was greatly strengthened by these various events. Once the United States had become the only really 'active' Power in the Middle East, not only the Middle Eastern governments basically hostile to Washington such as Cairo and Damascus, but also Baghdad and Amman found themselves in broad agreement. Both these last, though well disposed towards Washington, could not afford to neglect a cheap way of appeasing their public opinion. The same was even true of King Saud, who did want to appear less of a panarab champion than Nasser. Yet it was to Nasser and nobody else that the Arab people from the Nile to the Tigris and the Gulf of Oman gave their enthusiastic allegiance, now at its height.

Syria and Egypt were not slow to make the most of this turn of events. Official representatives of twenty-three African and Asian nations met in Cairo from October 21st to 23rd to make hurried plans for a full scale conference, while on October 31st the Council of the Arab League passed a unanimous resolution on solidarity with Syria. A congress of African and Asian jurists opened in Damascus on November 8th and in his inaugural address President Shukri Kuwatli contrived to link the Turco-Syrian crisis with the Israeli danger. A conference of Arab chambers of commerce, which was sponsored by the Arab League and opened in Cairo on November 23rd, considered the creation of an 'Arab common market' and an Arab shipping company which would carry the greater part of Arab oil (which was not in any case to be allowed to take any non-Arab land route). Finally, a major Arab oil conference, preceded by a meeting of experts in Baghdad, was to be held in 1958 with, if possible, the participation of delegates from the British protectorates in the Persian Gulf.

But Nasser's grand design was a 'new Bandung', a meeting to be held at the crossroads between two great and like-minded continents, where the emissaries of African and Asian governments and representatives of the peoples themselves would present a united front to Europe and to the 'battlefields' of the Middle East and the Maghreb. This was the theme of the Afro-Asian solidarity conference which took place in Cairo between December 26th, 1957, and January 1st, 1958. For the first time Moslems from the U.S.S.R. played an active part and were allotted a place in the permanent organs set up by the conference. Their attendance caused certain noteworthy abstentions; Turkey, Pakistan, the Philippines, South Vietnam and Cambodia were not there. But it secured for the Soviet 'big brother' a magnificent opening for propaganda to and patronage of the under-developed countries. The conference was likewise an admirable opportunity for the Arab peoples, especially Syria and Egypt, to make the most of their 'weapons' – political neutralism and non-alignment – and their immediate aspirations – revision of oil agreements and nationalization of major foreign enterprises. The organs created by the conference, consisting of a permanent secretariat and a solidarity committee, were established in Cairo.

At the beginning of 1958 there was no denying the real progress of the Arab peoples towards solidarity. Moscow vaunted it, Washington was worried by it, and the West was slow to recognize its extent because over simplified ideas about the chronic divisions of the Middle East still governed Western thinking. The movement produced quick results which took the West by surprise. These results were strange and although their ultimate causes are clear enough, their immediate causes remain obscure.

On February 1st, 1958, the Syrian President, Shukri Kuwatli, fulfilling a secret decision of the Syrian parliament of January 14th, signed an agreement in Cairo with President Nasser for the fusion of Syria and Egypt into a United Arab Republic. Surprise is legitimate; the agreement was concluded by one of the most uncompromising upholders of Syrian independence; it united two countries with no common frontier and with competing rather than complementary economies, but to quote the words of a first class Italian observer, Signore Paolo Minganti: 'However illogical from a practical point of view, the idea of a union between Syria and Egypt fulfilled every theoretical and ideological requirement.' The Syrian constitution of September 5th, 1950, had already declared that 'the people of Syria ... as a part of the Arab nation, look forward to the day when Syria will be part of a single Arab state', and this conception was at the heart of the Baath's thinking. The wish for such a union had been expressed by the Syrian parliament as far back as July 5th, 1957, and in specific fields it had been realized by the military agreement of October 20th, 1955, and the economic agreement of September 3rd, 1957.

During the winter of 1957–58 the idea of union with Egypt had fluctuating, and sometimes conflicting, repercussions on different sections of Syrian opinion, but the net effect was favourable to the current of Arab solidarity, then in full flood, and to the growing prestige of President Nasser. The patriots and nationalists of Damascus saw a better chance of preserving Syria's entity by a union with distant Egypt than by continuing to run the risk of absorption into a Fertile Crescent run by Iraq. They hoped to escape being done to death between the Iraqi and Jordanian jaws of the Hashemite vice and instead to open up for themselves exciting prospects of exerting pressure on Jordan, where public opinion was on their side, and on Lebanon, in which they could awaken Moslem nostalgia. Although Syria would be no more than a province in a wider Arab amalgam, it could now at the same time become a Greater Syria on its own account.

The Baath socialists saw in union a way of keeping their movement alive and themselves predominant in Syria without abandoning their principles or their social ideas, which were similar to Egypt's. In the same breath they hoped to exorcize the danger from the left which was being worked up by the great bourgeois red, Khaled al-Azm. Between this last and Shukri Kuwatli there was such intense personal rivalry that the old nationalist campaigner agreed to make a 'noble and startling sacrifice' on the altar of Arab unity by fulsome recognition of Nasser's primacy rather than risk defeat at the hands of a despised and hated adversary. Finally, the moderates and the 'haves' regarded the introduction of Egyptian legislation in Syria as the surest way of defeating the communist party.

Thus Syrians of varying outlook, some exercised by one danger and some by another, were drawn together by this central idea. Some, in private, were loath to go beyond federation, but in the end fusion emerged from a confusion of bids and overbids. Lukewarmness was immediately and fittingly eclipsed in an aura of heroism, and according to the communiqué issued in Cairo the statesmen there assembled 'had resolved that union, which is the logical goal for panarabism, is the right road to freedom and sovereignty for the Arabs and one of the means available to man to achieve collaboration and peace. It was therefore their duty to apply all the energy and persistence at their command to the task of translating such a union from the region of hope into that of hard fact.'

With the conclusion of the Cairo agreement Western observers, aware by now of Moscow's importance, were on the watch for Russian reactions. Contradictions abounded. On January 29th the U.S.S.R. agreed to an extensive technical aid agreement with Egypt; at the same moment the communist member of parliament for Damascus, Khaled Baghdash, fled his country as it passed into the ambit of Egyptian law. The U.S.S.R. evidently intended to play on the broad general currents of Middle Eastern nationalism rather than rely on Marxist propaganda and local agents.

The Russian press, which was cautious about adopting a line on Egyptian-Syrian fusion, continued to favour the movement for Arab unity but treated it as a domestic matter which concerned only Arab peoples and governments; it gave encouragement but strictly from the sidelines. What mattered first and foremost to the Russians was to prevent the Middle East from becoming a base available for Western use. Its hostility to the Baghdad Pact was as great as ever, but the blame for this diplomatic venture was laid on its British and American protagonists while the Middle Eastern members were pitied rather than chided for letting themselves get caught by such tactics. The U.S.S.R. was looking for friends, not allies. Everything suggested that Moscow was as usual waiting patiently for Washington to make fresh mistakes in a new and disconcerting situation.

From April 29th to May 16th President Nasser was on a visit to the U.S.S.R. which took him to the Moslem parts of central Asia. On his return to Moscow an unusually long joint communiqué proclaimed the will of the two countries to live peacefully side by side in spite of the differences between their systems of government and announced agreement on a great number of problems ('imperialist aggression' against Yemen, Algeria, Chinese representation in the United Nations, the rights of the Palestine Arab refugees, etc.) and their desire to develop economic and cultural co-operation. The United Arab Republic thanked the U.S.S.R. for help in industrialization, and the document ended with a plea for a summit conference. It is pertinent to recall that President Nasser's visit to Moscow was preceded by a noticeable improvement in the relations between the United Arab Republic and the United States, especially in economic and financial matters. The Egyptian dictator seemed to be winning on both fronts.

For the other Arab countries the creation of the United Arab Republic was obviously an event of the first importance. As might have been expected, official and popular reactions were many and various; they dominated the ensuing months.

On the official plane the first reaction came from Yemen which hurriedly opened negotiations and entered into a federal union with the United Arab Republic on March 8th. Social considerations certainly played no part in this move but the imam presumably hoped to secure a counterpoise to the pressure which the British exerted from Aden. The attitude of Saudi

Arabia was more ambiguous. The authorities in Syria maintained that King Saud had instigated a plot to kill Nasser, but the King's brother, emir Feisal, whose pro-Nasser proclivities were well known, succeeded on March 23rd in forcing the King to give him the full substance of the authority already delegated to him and, having taken the reins, gave Saudi policy an Egyptian twist. In Washington the Department of State seemed anxious to make light of this development and observed that there were no grounds for considering Feisal anti-American. Nevertheless a good deal had happened since King Saud's visit to the United States little more than a year before.

In Syria itself the practical effects of union were not unattended by difficulties, the whole range of which was not easy to assess but which were beyond a doubt. Economic adjustments were full of snags and were wisely undertaken slowly; some aspects of Egyptianization gave offence in Damascus. The Baath zealots who had contrived the union were disappointed to find that they did not enjoy Cairo's favour to the exclusion of everybody else; and Cairo made closer acquaintance with the changeable ways of the Syrians, who seemed half-inclined to preserve or even recover a certain degree of autonomy.

Neither Baghdad nor Amman tried to conceal its disgruntlement at the birth of the United Arab Republic, although Baghdad had the courtesy, or the shrewdness, to congratulate Nasser. But one ex-Prime Minister, Fadhi Jamali, who had always been a keen champion of the Iraqi brand of panarabism and was still very influential, immediately insisted that the Egyptian-Syrian union was 'abnormal and unnatural', whereas an Iraqi-Syrian union would have been the natural thing; Nuri's team could never forget the Fertile Crescent and Greater Syria.

It is hardly necessary to point out that oil was one of Baghdad's worries. By getting control of Syria President Nasser had gained possession of every land and sea outlet for Middle Eastern crude oil destined for Europe. This development lent special point to a suggestion made by Nuri a few months earlier for a return to the United Nations' 1947 plan for partitioning Palestine; this would have made it possible for oil to flow from Baghdad to Amman and Acre along an Arab land route under Hashemite control. But a return to that plan was no more than a flight of the imagination in view of the inevitable opposition of Israel, which moreover contemplated the Egyptian-Syrian fusion with astonishing equanimity and even refrained from debating it in parliament.

But the Hashemite monarchies produced a positive answer to the initiative taken by Cairo and Damascus. And the answer, as though to illustrate the strength of the movement for Arab unity, took the same form: the two Hashemite kings, Feisal and Hussein, federated their states on February 14th as an 'Arab Union', whose affairs would to all intents and purposes be in the hands of Nuri al-Said. The purely governmental nature of this union made it but a pale copy, quickly to be proved insubstantial, of the United Arab Republic.

Throughout the Arab world the popular cry, often raised to fever pitch by Cairo's 'Voice of the Arabs' broadcasts, was all for the United Arab Republic and there were popular demonstrations in shiite Hermil in Lebanon, in Jordan, in Jerusalem, Nablus and Salt, in Kuwait and at various places in Iraq. President Nasser's popularity soared afresh at this first practical step, under his aegis, towards realization of the zenith of Arab desires. These high-flown sentiments (which, paradoxically, were not irrelevant to a worsening of the situation in Cyprus and so to a serious problem for Nato), produced almost at once two acute crises, one in Lebanon and another in Iraq.

Trouble had been brewing in Lebanon since the spring. Noisy partisans of the United Arab Republic created disturbances at Tyre on March 28th and in the Shuf on April 9th. In the end the explosion was touched off by the assassination in Beirut on the night of May 7th–8th of a leading opposition journalist, Nassib Metni. As has already been described, matters in Lebanon were complicated by the interaction of factional and personal politics with the broad issues of Arab and even world affairs.

The Americans hesitated for a long time before intervening.

They were worried by the complexities of Lebanese politics and the probable reactions of Lebanese nationalists and they may have harboured the comfortable thought that they had no need to parade the Sixth Fleet but only to let it be known that they might do so. But indirect pressure was without effect and, acknowledging this fact, they finally decided to land troops on July 16th, by which time the repercussions of the Iraqi revolution had led them to fear for the life of President Chamoun.

Meanwhile the popular Arab tide had swept to its abrupt victory in Baghdad on the deliberately symbolic date of July 14th. There was some surprise at the overthrow of the Iraqi monarchy by a military coup, since the army had effectively proved its support of the established order in November 1952, but the event merely served to demonstrate the extent of the subsequent revulsion of feeling against the 'government of pashas'. The masses and the middle classes had made common cause and had thereby put a new face on the panarab movement.

Like the Americans at Beirut and for the same reasons, the British sent troops to Amman. They could not turn a deaf ear to King Hussein's appeal. Moreover, there is no doubt whatever that they expected this display of determination to put heart into their last friends and allies in the Middle East. By rallying to the support of the Jordanian throne, they aimed at securing their hold on Kuwait, for they were under no illusions about the underground workings of pro-Nasser sentiment among the sixty thousand inhabitants of the tiny principality that was responsible for one-third of the oil production of the Middle East and enabled Britain to keep itself supplied with sterling oil.

Anglo-Saxon interventions of this type could have no future. Once the immediate objects had been achieved the troops would have to be withdrawn without (if this were possible) compromising the people who had been saved by intervention. There was, however, a more serious consideration. The acts of intervention had branded Western, or rather Anglo-Saxon, policy with a character which, though inspired by the will to resist the U.S.S.R., could not fail to appear hostile to the new trends in the Arab world.

Thus Soviet interference, which had been a major factor in the Middle East from the autumn of 1955, was still shaping the future. It had undoubtedly been a dominating factor for a period of about two and a half years – years of capital importance in the evolution of this part of the world. Following the Palestine drama (which was still smouldering, though it had for a time taken second place), it had brought the popular movement for Arab unity to fruition and this movement, now clearly revealed in its new form, seemed bound to overshadow the immediate future. But as will be seen, events were to expose the weak spots in Arab unity as well as illustrate the agility and doggedness of Russian policy.

EPILOGUE

THE MIDDLE EAST IN THE SHADOW OF ASIA

The Middle East in the shadow of Asia

THE MIDDLE EAST crisis of 1958 reached its zenith in the events of July 14th–16th. For a moment, when the West accepted its responsibilities, there loomed the danger of a clash between the two world blocks as to who was to dominate, or, to use a less old-fashioned expression, to take the lead in the Levant.

But the moment passed and in a matter of days it became clear that there was to be no trial of strength. The Anglo-Saxons, by now realizing the consequences of their stand, drew back and set about limiting the political repercussions of an enterprise which had begun to look distinctly hazardous. The Russians denounced 'imperialist' aggression as a matter of course but instead of pressing on to the point of challenge, merely tried to start a general palaver. Out of this, no doubt, they hoped to get official recognition of their right to intervene in Middle Eastern affairs – a right which, in fact, they had already secured. From there, they hoped to move on to some summit conference at which the Great in concert would settle Middle Eastern affairs.

But this prospect too vanished. The sequence of events suggests that before the preliminary moves were over the U.S.S.R. was called to order by its Chinese ally. From Peking's point of view there was more to be said against than for a settlement of purely Middle Eastern problems, since the imperialists had to be brought to terms in the Pacific and not merely in the Mediterranean. All of a sudden, Russian diplomatic activity petered out, Chinese batteries opened heavy fire on Quemoy, American attention was immediately diverted to the Far East, and on August 19th, 1958, the Lebanese daily paper, *L'Orient*, entitled its leader 'From Beirut to Peking'.

So the idea of a summit conference was dropped. Once more the United Nations was left to map out a settlement in the Middle East. In these circumstances, this could only be of limited scope – concentration on a few essentials, the re-establishment of the formal *status quo* and the preservation of a shaky balance within the two countries, Jordan and Lebanon, whose affairs had led to foreign intervention. It soon became obvious that the Anglo-Saxons had no chance of securing the adoption of a resolution to their taste, one which would tacitly condemn and check Nasserite ambitions. 'Neutral' delegations proposed compromise drafts without much hope of securing the necessary two-thirds majority.

The Arabs made good use of the Chinese diversion which, designedly or not, gave Asian solidarity a touch of reality. They set out to insulate Middle Eastern affairs against all external influence. On August 20th the members of the Arab League (together with Morocco and Tunisia which joined the League soon afterwards) put forward a resolution which for all practical purposes left the pacification of the Middle East in their hands. For the observer of forms (and what other guide is there in such a case?) the heated debate that followed was pointless, since the crisis was on the wane. The Arab resolution was carried unanimously and the Secretary-General, Mr. Dag Hammarskjöld, once more took up his pilgrim's staff and set out for the Middle East with instructions to see it implemented.

The West had intervened in July on behalf of two members of the Arab League which, rightly or wrongly, believed themselves threatened by their neighbours and allies, and this intervention made plain the fact that the Arab world was divided. Five weeks later the Arabs had closed their ranks sufficiently to produce an agreed solution of their own for the crisis and to get their plan accepted by the United Nations. This was a skilful manœuvre and by it the Arab League, which had been out of mind since the Baghdad Pact crisis, gained a new lease of international life. President Nasser, converted overnight from culprit to mediator, found his prestige greatly enhanced.

The Arab resolution was cleverly framed; it took account of all the opinions that had come to light during the crisis; it also referred to the principles, expressed or implied, on the basis of which a settlement had already been reached. It took up the Russian phrase on the withdrawal of foreign troops, though it watered down 'without delay' to 'shortly'; from President Eisenhower's inaugural address it borrowed the idea of a development authority to be 'directed by the Arab States themselves' and bolstered with outside aid; by entrusting the study of this plan to the Secretary-General of the U.N. it removed it from the range of Great Power pressures; lastly, by putting Mr. Hammarskjöld in charge of restoring order in Jordan and Lebanon, it contrived to maintain the Arab League's stand on non-intervention.

For the resolution of August 21st – and herein lies its considerable skill – expressly recognized the virtues of the League and sanctified the principles (laid down in article 8 of its charter) of non-interference in the internal affairs of member states and respect for their established systems of government. The Arabs were spared the warnings, however tactfully worded, of the Norwegian resolution enjoining abstention and were allowed to record their 'renewed assurances' of non-interference as though there had never been any question of this. Instead of laying plans for settling the crisis, the resolution denied that there had ever been one. It thus cut the ground from under the feet of those who laid the blame on agents of the United Arab Republic, and indirectly justified President Nasser's policies. It recognized the Arabs' exclusive right to manage their own affairs.

And yet this diplomatic feat attracted admiration rather than assent. The move was a clever one, even too clever. There was no concealing the artificiality of the display of solidarity that ended so patent a crisis; agreements as sudden and as loudly proclaimed seldom have solid roots.

The League's classic function seems to be to draw a veil over Arab dissensions – even to keep them dark; its reappearance on the international scene was therefore enacted in time-honoured style. But experienced observers are not taken in. The one element that might give its protestations new meaning and even some practical effect is the sense of solidarity which has long been at work among the Arab peoples despite the manœuvres of their governments – and from which President Nasser alone has so far profited. The clue to the question whether these popular emotions still work for his benefit alone is to be found not in New York, but in the Middle East itself.

At the end of that U.N. session President Nasser seemed to the world at large to be more than ever the arbiter of the Arab world. This impression was heightened when Mr. Hammarskjöld went to Cairo, after failing to evolve in Amman a formula which would both enable the British paratroopers to withdraw and leave King Hussein safe on his throne. It was clear that if there were a solution, only Nasser could produce it.

And so it transpired, for the British decided to evacuate, and finished doing so on October 30th. But although the facts were there for all to see, the inner workings remained matter for conjecture. Since there was no expansion either of the strength or the role of the U.N. forces in the Middle East, how was King Hussein's position assured? The prospective arrival of a few U.N. diplomats was obviously not the equivalent for this purpose of a brigade, and it began to look as if the best guarantee of King Hussein's throne was the confusion which his fall would entail. In particular, how ignore Israeli claims if Jordan were to be partitioned? It was not in the interests of the Arab states to allow this question to arise in the immediate future and in these circumstances President Nasser may well have given some sort of a guarantee of the *status quo* in Jordan, receiving in return for his good offices certain guarantees from King Hussein. But this again is conjecture, leaving observers far from sure about the future behaviour of the United Arab Republic or about Jordan's fate.

In Lebanon the position was clearer. The Lebanese settled their own affairs, though not without troubles which, in the first days of October, almost wrecked the calm that reigned after the elections of July 31st, and even jeopardized the very survival of the state. On the one hand President Chamoun took the view that there was no need for him to lay down his office before his legal term expired on September 23rd and in the interim the authority of the president elect, General Shehab, naturally suffered. On the other hand President Shehab, when finally confirmed in office in September, did not feel able to appoint a 'neutral' Prime Minister, as he had been expected to do, but called on the leader of the rising in Tripoli, Rashid Keramé. This choice was interpreted as a challenge by yesterday's loyalists, now the opposition, who rallied round the outgoing President, Camille Chamoun and the leader of the Lebanese Falange, Pierre Jumayyil. The latter thereupon converted his party, which for thirty years had stood for Lebanese independence, into a Christian self-preservation group and started a minor insurrection which succeeded in paralysing the country by means of a strike.

After various fruitless attempts President Chehab finally succeeded on October 14th in assembling a balanced cabinet of the typical Lebanese kind. Pierre Jumayyil and Rashid Keramé were both members together with two less obviously partisan politicians, Raymond Eddé and Hussein Oueini. This cabinet contained perforce Moslems and Christians, though only Maronite Christians and Sunni Moslems. Urgent tasks awaited it – the easing of tempers, the disarmament of irregular formations, economic recovery – but would Parliament give it the necessary power? And how long could a parliament survive which had been elected in suspect circumstances and contained an opposition which felt that it had won a victory and then renounced the fruits? Yet how could an election be held in prevailing conditions? There was no end to pressing problems in Lebanon.

Meanwhile the American troops had completed their withdrawal by October 26th. Lebanon survived as a unit in its traditional form with its independence preserved, but the head of the government was self-avowedly pro-Nasser. Here again the President of the United Arab Republic had for the time being scored on points, even if he had not won a complete victory, and he might one day be tempted to consolidate his uncertain advantage.

Contrary to almost universal expectation, the United Arab Republic's set-back came not in Amman or Beirut but in Baghdad. Although the coup in Iraq was, like its forerunner in Egypt, a victory for nationalism and panarabism won by middle-class officers over a 'régime of pashas', the analogy was not as close as first appearances suggested. As Marcel Colombe puts it: 'The Egyptian revolution was directed against all-powerful political parties and was bound to move swiftly to a single-party system. The second (Iraqi) revolution was directed against the "dictatorship" of Nuri al-Said and made for the benefit of opposition parties and groups which had been persecuted by "despotic" pashas. Consequently a single-party system was *a priori* incompatible with the revolution.' In the event General Abdul Karim Kassem invited representatives of rival parties to join his government and allowed eminent exiles such as Rashid Ali el-Gaylani to return to Iraq, but he was slow to take a political line and restricted himself at first to paternalist measures for the relief of the poorer classes. Like Husni Zaim in Syria before him he set himself against hoarding and dear bread; a policy of marked Iraqi nationalism emerged only gradually. Early in October he removed Colonel Abdel Salem Aref, a champion of the merger of Iraq with the United Arab Republic, from the army and then from the government, and finally on November 4th had him arrested. Baath ministers were dismissed and Rashid Ali, who was too responsive to Nasser's appeal and perhaps also too much imbued with out-of-date ideas, was silenced. His eclipse was a measure of the course that events had run in the Middle East in less than twenty years.

The disappearance of Nuri al-Said was therefore no gain to Nasser but rather the reverse. His popularity and his policies had flourished so long as his chief enemy was a man hated by the people, but the hated tyrant's place in Baghdad had now been taken by a popular dictator who was no less resolved to keep

Iraq independent and who was immune to the propaganda which had done service to Nasser before the coup.

Under Kassem Iraq's chances improved in the competition for Arab leadership which Nasser had looked like winning. This was one of the effects of the Iraqi revolution. Another, as will be seen, was its impact on Russo-Arab relations.

History cannot be refashioned, even on paper, but it is tempting to think that if the Iraqi coup had happened six months earlier, Syria would have turned to Baghdad rather than Cairo to fulfil its craving for unity. This thought may have occurred to Nasser, as one among the many worries about his 'northern province'.

As if out of malice, the new Iraqi government added to these worries. Evidence given during the trials in Baghdad of leading members of the old order confirmed, if confirmation were needed, how consistently Iraq had sought the unification of the Fertile Crescent and also revealed how favourably the plan had often been entertained in Damascus. A Syrian nationalist like Sabry Assali, whom Nasser had made vice-president of the United Arab Republic, had been by no means unreceptive to this Iraqi brand of panarabism.

President Nasser was quick to seize the opportunity to remodel his government, making it more centralized and throwing out Assali. His problem was to keep tighter control of a 'northern province' which retained a lively sense of independence and made little attempt to hide its disappointment over the miserable economic results of the union with Egypt. By January 1959 this economic trend was causing alarm in Damascus and Aleppo. By September alarm had turned to bitterness.

Syria could be kept in check by riding it on a tight rein, but to do so scarcely increased Egypt's appeal for Syrians. On October 11th, 1958, the Tunisian delegate, who had just taken his seat as a new member of the Arab League, attacked Cairo's manœuvres in a speech which some delegates secretly relished, though they failed to back it.

If Egypt had chosen the opposite course and given Syria its

head the United Arab Republic might have moved towards a looser federation or confederation, to include an associated state of Yemen and a new autonomous Syrian entity and also in due course other states such as Kuwait, Jordan and even Iraq itself. Iraq's opposition was the principal obstacle to this development. Iraq gave President Nasser good reason to intensify his power in the areas already under his control, but it also exposed a decline in his powers of attraction. Time would show.

It would be easy to list other examples of Nasserite plans which turned out less well than expected. One such cropped up in an unduly neglected sector of the Middle East.

President Nasser's mind ranges beyond panarabism. He is mindful of the existence of a Kurdish population in the Syrian Jazirah in the extreme north-east of his 'northern province'. He knows that the Kurds cherish grievances against all the denizens of the Middle East except the Syrians – and the Russians. Early in June 1958 Cairo radio began broadcasting in Kurdish (Nasser evidently intended to play on Kurdish nationalism) and within a month results were noticeable in the Kurdish areas of Iraq and Iran as well as in Syria. On all sides, and particularly in Turkey, the fear grew that Nasser intended to create a 'satellite' Kurdish state wedged in between the members of the Baghdad Pact and linking the United Arab Republic with the U.S.S.R.

But immediately after the proclamation of the Iraqi republic General Kassem, who had included prominent Kurds in his Sovereignty Council and cabinet, promulgated a provisional constitution in which article 3 ran to the effect that Iraqi society was based upon the co-operation of all citizens and respect for their rights and liberties, that Arabs and Kurds belonged to this nation and the constitution guaranteed their national rights within the Iraqi entity. Kurdish leaders under sentence were amnestied and exiles like the famous Mullah Mustafa Barzani, who had fled to the Armenian S.S.R. after the collapse of the Kurdish republic of Mahabad, were allowed to return to Iraq and were given a warm welcome. The Kurdish press in Iraq at once and enthusiastically shifted its attention from cultural to political affairs and proposed the transformation of the country into a true federation between an Arab and a Kurdish unit.

Whatever it might think of such a plan, General Kassem's government was careful not to destroy a picture which might well appeal to the Kurds of the Syrian Jazirah and seduce them from Cairo's orbit into Baghdad's, thus aiding and abetting Iraq's long-term designs on Damascus. Paradoxically this Kurdish revival put new life into Nuri al-Said's cherished Arab plan for the Fertile Crescent. Thus the Kurdish question did Nasser no good, although it had been raised in the first place by Cairo radio.

But there was one country which was even better placed than Iraq to profit from the Kurdish situation. The Iranian government saw its opportunity and reacted to the first Cairo broadcasts by announcing a development programme for the Kurdish provinces of Iran and by starting Kurdish radio programmes of its own. The natural links, ethnic and linguistic, between Kurds and Persians could easily be made to play an extra part in the situation.

The revival of the Kurdish question could have unpredictable repercussions in the Middle East. From the point of view of the West the prospect is not necessarily alarming, since the West's Middle Eastern allies would gain in strength and stability if they had the sense to convert their Kurdish subjects into satisfied citizens. But there is also Moscow to consider; it has long posed as the friend of the Kurds, has acquired influence among them and will certainly try to turn any new development to its own advantage.

One of the surprises of the summer of 1958 was the postponement of a new crisis over Arab oil, expected ever since President Nasser's first proposal to hold an Arab oil conference.

The new Iraqi government belied the fears roused by the revolution of July 14th and seemed averse to any extreme measures which might kill the goose that laid the golden eggs. Anxious to boost the earnings which had been seriously reduced by the Suez crisis, Baghdad was intent upon increased production and an increase in its share of the proceeds. On the first point the Iraq Petroleum Company was in entire agreement with the Iraqi government and set about raising production to 60 million tons by 1961. On the second point the Company took the line that it would honour its obligations but wished to refer division of the proceeds to arbitration, pointing out that its own rates had not been exceeded by any other oil company.

On this topic, as in political matters, Iraq asserted its freedom to act independently of Nasser, and with minor variations the Rulers of Kuwait and Quatar and the Sheikh of Abu Dhabi (in whose domains British Petroleum and the Compagnie Française des Pétroles had recently discovered underwater reserves) did likewise. For the time being they prefer large, regular and punctual payments to the presentation of joint claims which would involve risking the bird in hand. The ruling fifty-fifty division has been undermined by offers from Signor Mattei and a number of Japanese and even some American firms; the local belief is that sooner or later the older producers can be brought into line in a series of individual and orthodox negotiations.

Kuwait, whose relations with Iraq had been strained, began to draw closer to Baghdad, to which it could offer a deep water port for the loading of the oil from the Basrah field. Meanwhile Iran, in the full flood of development in the new fields of Aga Jari and Gach Saran in the south-west and busy prospecting in Qum in central Iran, was working harmoniously with foreign associates and dreaming about the long pipe line through Turkey to Alexandretta which would enable it to export some of its future production without using the routes across the Arab world. There was therefore little common ground for the Middle Eastern oil conference which had figured in Nasser's dreams since 1956, and Cairo postponed its opening for the fifth time (until April 16th, 1959), possibly in the hope of stepping up Egyptian activity in the Gulf sheikhdoms.

Apart from a moment of stock-exchange panic on July 15th, 1958, in London and especially Paris (where the shares in the Compagnie Française des Pétroles fell by 26% in a single day –

but then gradually recovered the whole loss), the West views with equanimity the possible loss of Arab oil supplies. A survey undertaken in August by the periodical *Western World* among a dozen leading authorities on world oil showed that conditions of world supply were more favourable than in 1956; that the whole of Middle Eastern production could be made good from other 'unexplored potentialities'; that the problem of longer haul could be met in tankers which were then temporarily laid up; and that the loss of Arab oil, though a serious inconvenience, would be neither fatal nor permanent. For the rest, most of the experts consulted held that the Arab states would gain nothing by 'going on strike', since they could not themselves exploit their resources and they needed the earnings which only the West was minded to provide.

If it is true that in the Arab countries, particularly Egypt, passions speak louder than self-interest and that the Suez affair taught the Egyptian dictator that it is not only possible but even sometimes profitable to defy the West, the world position of oil nevertheless counsels caution and moderation to the oil-producing Arab states. The rate of growth in the consumption of petroleum products is slowing down and new sources of supply are beginning to appear. From now on there will be less harrying of oil companies and fewer threats of nationalization and more attempts to get immediate financial returns and to play a decisive part in oil policy. Such will be the negotiations and guiding considerations in agreements in the future.

The communists are not entirely out of the picture. Rumour at Teheran has it that the Russians will undertake to exploit the oilfields in return for a mere 10%. Nasser has confirmed that Arab oil technicians are being trained in Russia. Finally, even if the U.S.S.R. is not in a position to buy Arab oil, since it has enough oil of its own, Asia and particularly the rapidly industrializing China might be able to do so.

Russian technicians and Chinese purchasers could therefore together provide an answer. But such a possibility is as yet remote. At the moment the Arab states still prefer to come to an agreement with Western companies to manage their oilfields and increase their profits as much as possible in an unfavourable world situation.

Russian activity was restrained throughout the summer of 1958 but every turn in Arab affairs revealed the U.S.S.R. as ever present and sitting pretty. With its customary consideration for local sovereignty Moscow confined itself to denouncing intervention by other Powers, 'aggressive' pacts and military landings; it proposed round table conferences to remove misunderstandings and differences and did its best to give the peoples of the Middle East the impression that it was the ideal partner in their quest for aid and progress. Yet by the autumn, when the Middle East had resumed an air of peace and quiet, the Russians began to be more active. Within a matter of days a number of significant acts revealed their ambition to penetrate into the various countries of the area: an offer of financial and technical help in the construction of the Aswan high dam, the announcement of a forthcoming visit to Cairo by Mr. Krushchev, a warning to Teheran, and the ferment in extreme left-wing circles round the new government in Iraq.

The reopening of the question of the Aswan dam by the Russians on October 21st was a major event and may be as full of consequences for the Arab world as the announcement of Russian arms deliveries on September 27th, 1955. The withdrawal of American offers to help finance the high dam, as is known, excited the greatest resentment in Egypt. At that time the Russians did not think fit to define or revive their own proposals; no doubt they were waiting for fresh disturbances to prepare the ground for them. By 1958 they may have felt the time had come.

Fortified by this offer, the Egyptians turned their attention to a radical transformation of their agriculture, which would be made possible by the elimination of dependence on the annual rise of the Nile and the immense increase in the area of cultivable land. They plan to commit their economy for half a century ahead. Whether or not they are acting rashly, the Russians are bound to profit. If and when the work is completed, they will get the credit for having started it and their propagandists will know how to make the most of this advantage; if on the other hand the plan has to be abandoned or cut down, the odium will be pinned on the West for refusing or haggling over aid.

The Kremlin began to press home its psychological advantage. Mr. Krushchev, it was announced, would visit the capital of the United Arab Republic in December and attend the Afro-Asian economic conference. He was assured of a most enthusiastic reception.

Russian favours, however, were not showered exclusively on the 'Egyptian province'. The Russian technical aid programme was extended to the 'Syrian province' where it fostered hopes which were all the greater because of the anxiety caused by the economic crisis. It also included Lebanon which had been severely hit by recent events and was said to have received tempting offers. At the same time Moscow issued warnings to those Middle Eastern states which it suspected of seeking closer ties with the West; Iran, for example, whose weaknesses were well known in the Kremlin, was advised on October 31st not to enter into a new and close military agreement with the United States. Finally, extreme left-wing elements in the new Iraqi republic became increasingly active as the Baath and pro-Nasser factions fell under a cloud. The left seemed to be attaining a dominant position and Baghdad had to face the alternatives of a Popular Democracy or anarchy.

Yet the United Arab Republic remains for outsiders the typical example of a Middle Eastern government seduced by Soviet totalitarianism. It was attacked in the Arab League at the beginning of October by Tunisia – the newest member – when President Bourguiba accused Cairo not only of giving aid and asylum to his opponent, Salah Ben Yussef, convicted of treason, but also of trying to establish an unjustifiable and even a personal dictatorship over the whole Arab world. The Tunisian President went further still in a speech to his own Constituent Assembly on October 16th when he pilloried the association between the United Arab Republic and the U.S.S.R. He addressed the men in power in Cairo as follows :

'A two-tier policy of co-operating with Russia and suppressing domestic Communism will not lead any of us astray. It is an impossible gambit. Russia is the stay of Communism throughout the world and does not try to conceal it. No one believes that the Russians are prepared to deliver arms to a country and at the same time countenance imprisonment of that country's Communists. The truth is that infiltration takes place gradually; only when you are well and truly hooked do you realize what Communism involves. I put this bluntly. I add that, if the worst were to come to the worst, we could side with you in a quarrel with the Americans. This is because we are free to do so. You know this from your own experience since you have co-operated with them and you were able to turn to them to secure the withdrawal of the British troops. What I fear now is that you will not be able to do the same again once things have gone wrong and, disappointed, you want to take up with the Americans again. When the iron curtain falls, all is over. History offers no case of a country which has been able to come back from behind it. Central Europe bears witness to this.'

This warning to the Egyptian dictator from the head of an Arab state caused the liveliest satisfaction among the Anglo-Saxons, though they may have overlooked the fact that Nasser was not the only Arab leader with an eye on Moscow, just as he was no longer the only focus for Arab unity. For Baghdad is pursuing a policy which is independent of, and could become hostile to, that of Cairo.

Meanwhile the U.S.S.R. intends to play both sides. It is confident that it can take advantage in the future of bickering between Arabs just as in the past it contrived to exploit Western mistakes and Western differences with the Middle East. While the Arabs have been able to throw off Western imperialism they cannot claim to have achieved unity among themselves. It would appear that the U.S.S.R., its prestige increased and its position strengthened by the invaluable aid given to Cairo and Baghdad, felt able to manipulate these two rivals without having to give preference to either. It remains to be seen whether this policy of 'divide and rule', which in the light of past experience the Arabs shrewdly mistrust, can be sustained, and whether the Russians can indefinitely avoid making an awkward choice between the '*frères ennemis*' of the Arab world.

One final word : when this book was being finished, the abiding question still remained : what today is *the* Eastern Question? More precisely, is the era of Soviet intervention over or not? Has Arab unity sufficient impetus to bring about a new era and become the dominant theme of the future?

It still holds the stage and its core is still the Nasser legend, but Nasser may prove to have been but an episode in the full story. His very success, greater in the minds of men than in fact, has started counter-currents, ruffled pride here and interests there, and raised up imitators who are liable to become rivals. Nothing could be less predictable than his future, though it would be rash to reckon upon his approaching eclipse or to believe that his fall would radically alter the course of events. Disorder and chaos in the Middle East will not end with him, for these things have their roots deep in the past; they include the existence of Israel (though this fact is less in the limelight at the moment), hatred of 'imperialism', distrust of the West, and a whole series of mistakes by Europeans and above all by Americans. There will never be any lack of people to voice and make capital out of these emotions.

This chronic restlessness would be less worrying if it were not used by the U.S.S.R. as a pretext for political action and a means to political ends. Russian intervention waxes and wanes; for years it was not exercised; suddenly it became overwhelming; at other times it is so veiled as to be practically forgotten. It was so during the summer of 1958, from the time of the collapse of the Russian plan for a summit conference until the renewal of the Russian offer for the high dam at Aswan which marked the revival, or rather the continuity, of Russian aims.

Russian intervention both exploits and fosters panarabism. 'For two years,' President Nasser told a Lebanese journalist in August 1958, 'the Russians have not refused a single Arab request'; and René Aggiouri wrote in a leader in the Beirut paper, *L'Orient*, on August 24th: 'Nasserism may be no more than the self-confidence which Nasser has given to the Arabs. This confidence needed, for its fruition, to be matched by an equal confidence among foreigners. The Russians were clever enough to be the first to show this confidence.' This description needs to be expanded, for it is not only the Russians but the whole communist world from Prague to Peking that accords sympathy and material help to the Arabs in the Middle East. Thus the great mass of central Asia and the Far East now impinges on its western promontory of Asia Minor and the Levant and on their African neighbours.

Westerners are amazed and alarmed at the magnitude of these events. They behold the inflation of the Nasser legend, the boundless visions of panarabism, the immoderate boldness and arrogance of the Kremlin, and the immense achievements and vast ambitions of Peking. Here, in the words of Gobineau but in modern form, is the 'mass of perils which Asia is piling up to break on the head of Europe', perils which they, like he, do well to heed.

We must hope that this vigilance will be directed to serious reflection and methodical labours instead of being consumed in useless worry. The voice of worldly wisdom can be heard in the heart of Asia among the ancient Kurdish people whose reawakening has been noted. It speaks comfort to men of peace, denouncing the excesses of despots in old sayings which may cheer us on our way: 'Things break when they shrink, men when they swell.' So much for Pride which disdains the bounds ordained by God. And for Artifice which thinks it can overcome every obstacle: 'None is slyer than the fox but his skin is in every market place.'

APPENDIXES

I. TABLE OF PRINCIPAL DATES 1859–1958

1859 April: Ferdinand de Lesseps inaugurates work on the Suez Canal at Port Said.

1861 June 9th: Mount Lebanon becomes an autonomous province of the Ottoman empire. Modified in 1864, the statute remains in force until unilaterally abrogated by the Turks at the beginning of the first World War.

1869 First Young Turk newspaper published in London.
November 17th: the Suez canal opened to traffic.

1872 The reformer Janal ad-Din al-Afghani settles in Cairo.

1878 March 3rd: the Turks sign the treaty of San Stefano after the Russian armies have been halted by the Powers at the gates of Constantinople.
June 4th: Cyprus pledged to Great Britain in return for a guarantee of the Asian frontiers of the Ottoman empire.

1881 December 20th: the Sultan submits to the creation of a Council for the Ottoman Public Debt, consisting of representatives of foreign creditors.

1882 July 15th: the British land at Alexandria and occupy Egypt.

1888 October 29th: an international convention, signed at Constantinople, guarantees the right of free passage through the Suez canal.

1894 Young Turk Committee of Union and Progress formed in Paris.

1897 August 24th: Zionist congress at Basle demands the establishment in Palestine of a home for the Jewish people secured by public law.

1898 Rashid Rida founds the reformist review *Al Manar*.

1899 January 23rd: Treaty consolidating British tutelage over Kuwait.

1903 March 5th: Germany obtains from the Porte the concession for the Baghdad railway.

Le reveil de la nation arabe published in Paris by Neguib Azuri.

1907 August 31st : Anglo-Russian agreement on zones of influence in Iran.

1908 William Knox d'Arcy strikes oil in southern Iran.

July 23rd : the Young Turks seize power in Constantinople and force the Sultan to restore the constitution.

1909 April 14th : formation of the Anglo-Persian Oil Company.

1913 May 30th : Turkey signs preliminaries of peace in London after its defeat by the Balkan coalition.

June 18th : meeting in Paris of the first Arab National Congress.

1914 October 30th : the Ottoman empire enters the war on the side of the Central Powers.

November 5th : Cyprus becomes a British colony.

November 23rd : the Sultan-Caliph at Constantinople proclaims a Holy War.

December 18th : Great Britain assumes protectorate over Egypt.

1915 March 4th : Anglo-Franco-Russian agreement for the partition of the Middle East into zones of administration and influence.

July 14th : political exchanges begin between Sherif Hussein of Mecca and the British High Commissioner in Egypt, Sir Henry MacMahon. Continued until January 30th, 1916.

August 21st : Lebanese patriots executed at Beirut by the Turks.

1916 February 19th : Tripartite convention implements the agreement of March 4th, 1915.

May 16th : Sykes-Picot agreement outlines Anglo-French division of the Arab Middle East.

June 10th : Sherif Hussein addresses a declaration of independence to the commander of the Turkish garrison in Mecca and (June 27th) issues a proclamation justifying his revolt.

November 6th : Sherif Hussein proclaims himself King of the Arabs.

1917 August 21st : convention of Saint-Jean-de-Maurienne awards Italy a sphere of influence in western Anatolia.

November 2nd : Britain enunciates the Balfour Declaration,

promising the establishment in Palestine of a National Home for the Jewish people.

1918 October 30th: the Allied Powers impose the armistice of Mudros on the defeated Ottoman empire.

November 13th: Saad Zaghlul and the Wafd claim independence for Egypt.

1919 January 29th: Emir Feisal asks the Peace Conference for independence for the Arabic-speaking people of Asia.

May 15th: Greek forces land at Smyrna.

1920 April 18th–25th: the San Remo agreements transfer Mosul and Palestine to British influence and place Syria and Lebanon under French, Palestine under British, mandate.

June 1st: the United States Senate refuses a mandate over Armenia.

July 25th: French troops evict King Feisal from Damascus.

August 10th: the Treaty of Sèvres between the Allied Powers and Turkey creates an independent Armenia and reduces France's projected sphere of influence in southern Anatolia.

September 1st: a considerably enlarged Lebanon becomes a distinct political entity (greater Lebanon) due for independence.

November 29th: proclamation of the Socialist Soviet Republic of Armenia within the U.S.S.R.

1921 January 20th: Emir Feisal claims Palestine for the independent Arab zone.

March 12th: Britain's Arab policy defined at the Cairo conference, presided over by Winston Churchill.

March 16th: Russo-Turkish treaty signed in Moscow.

May 1st: Arabs and Zionists in bloody disturbances in Jaffa.

August 23rd: Feisal I ascends the throne in Baghdad.

October 20th: the Ankara agreement between France and Kemalist Turkey provides for reduction of France's sphere of influence and withdrawal of Syrian frontier to a point on the Gulf of Alexandretta.

1922 February 28th: Britain recognizes Egyptian independence subject to continued British military occupation and to British reservations covering, in particular, imperial communications and defence.

June 3rd: Winston Churchill declares that Palestine will not be turned into a Jewish National Home but that a National Home will be established there.

September 9th: Kemalist forces recapture Smyrna and put an end to the Greek adventure in Anatolia.

September 16th: Transjordan is detached from Palestine, excepted from the 'zionist articles' of the mandate and converted into an emirate for Abdullah.

October 10th: Anglo-Iraqi treaty regulating Britain's mandatory powers.

1923 May 25th: Transjordan is declared independent under Emir Abdullah, subject to a discreet form of British protection.

October 29th: Turkey proclaimed a republic.

1924 October 30th: King Hussein evicted from Mecca by ibn Saud, and drops his newly assumed style and title of caliph.

1925 July 24th: revolt in Syria against the French mandatory.

December 16th: the League of Nations allots the vilayet of Mosul to Iraq.

1926 January 8th: union of Hedjaz and Nejd under ibn Saud, which in 1932 becomes the Kingdom of Saudi-Arabia.

1927 October 25th: important strike of oil near Kirkuk in northern Iraq.

1928 February 20th: Anglo-Transjordan agreement redefines Britain's tutelage; a non-parliamentary constitution for Transjordan is granted on April 16th.

1929 August 23rd: 249 deaths in Palestine as the result of an Arab-Jewish affray at the Wailing Wall.

1930 June 30th: Anglo-Iraqi treaty emancipates Iraq.

1931 December 6th: opening of an islamic congress in Jerusalem held on the initiative of Haj Amin al Husseini.

1932 July 18th: admission of Kemalist Turkey to the League of Nations.

October 3rd: admission of Iraq to the League of Nations.

1933 August 11th: massacre of Assyrian Christians in northern Iraq.

September 8th: death of King Feisal I of Iraq in Berne.

1936 January 20th: grave riots in Syria against the French mandate.

April 15th: murder of two Jews by Arabs marks the beginning of serious and sustained disturbances in Palestine.

July 20th: Turkey obtains at Montreux a new settlement of the Straits, which are in effect put under Turkish control.

August 26th: Anglo-Egyptian treaty completely liberates Egypt except for the British right to garrison the Suez Canal Zone and to use the territory in time of war.

October 9th: Franco-Syrian treaty initialled (signed December 22nd).

October 29th: Bakr Sidki and Hikmat Sulaiman institute a dictatorship in Iraq.

November 13th: signature of Franco-Lebanese treaty due to put an end to the mandate.

1937 January 5th: under the revived constitution of 1926 Lebanon achieves a division of its highest offices between a Maronite President and a Sunni Prime Minister.

March 26th: Egypt admitted to the League of Nations.

July 7th: the report of the Peel Commission recommends the partition of Palestine.

July 8th: Turkey, Iraq, Iran and Afghanistan sign the Saadabad Pact.

August 11th: murder of the dictator Bakr Sidki at Mosul.

1938 August 2nd: completion of the trans-Iranian railway.

November 9th: the British government lays before Parliament the Woodhead report on the partition of Palestine and declares partition impracticable.

November 10th: death of Mustapha Kemal at Istanbul.

December 14th: the French government withdraws the Franco-Syrian and Franco-Lebanese treaties from Parliament.

1939 March 31st: the Taurus railway reaches Mosul.

May 17th: a British White paper restricts Zionist immigration into Palestine to 75,000 persons over five years and proposes the establishment of an Arab-Jewish state in Palestine within ten years.

June 23rd: the sanjak of Alexandretta is ceded to Turkey and becomes the Hatay.

October 19th: Treaty of Mutual Assistance between Britain, France and Turkey.

1941 May 2nd: Rashid Ali's revolt in Iraq against the British.

May 29th: Anthony Eden revives Britain's Arab policy by his Mansion House speech, on the morrow of the Iraqi rising.

June 8th : British and Free French forces enter Syria and Lebanon which had remained loyal to Vichy.

August 7th : the Lyttelton–de Gaulle exchange of letters confirms the preservation of predominant French interests in Syria and Lebanon.

August 25th : British and Russian occupation of Iran.

September 28th–November 26th : General Catroux proclaims Lebanon's, and later Syria's, right to independence.

November : Britain establishes the Middle East Supply Centre.

1942 January 29th : tripartite treaty of alliance between Iran, Britain and Russia.

February 4th : the British force King Farouk to appoint Nahas Pasha Prime Minister.

October 23rd : Egypt freed from the threat of German-Italian occupation by the British victory at El Alamein.

1943 November 8th : the Lebanese government of Bishara al-Khuri and Riyad as-Solh denounces the mandatory provisions of the constitution of 1926 and for practical purposes puts an end to the mandate.

November 21st : following a French attempt to retrieve the position, the Khuri-Solh government is restored and accepts the 'national pact'.

December 22nd : France begins to hand over to the Syrian and Lebanese governments.

1944 August 2nd : Turkey breaks off diplomatic relations with Germany.

October 7th : signature of the Alexandria protocol by the Arab states of the Middle East.

October 8th : dismissal of Nahas Pasha.

1945 January 31st : eastern orthodox prelates invited to the council convened in Moscow for the election of a patriarch.

February 23rd : Turkish declaration of war on Germany.

March 22nd : Pact of the Arab League, signed by Egypt, Iraq, Syria, Lebanon, Transjordan, Saudi Arabia and Yemen.

May 6th : anti-French rising in Damascus.

May 30th : the French are compelled by the British to cease their opposition to the Syrian rising.

December 13th : Franco-British agreement for the evacuation of Syria and Lebanon.

December 20th : the Egyptian government raises the issue of the Anglo-Egyptian treaty of 1936.

1946 October 4th : President Truman endorses the Jewish Agency's aspiration for a Jewish state in a viable area of Palestine.

1947 February 14th : Britain refers the Palestine problem to the United Nations.

March 12th : the Truman Doctrine of aid for Greece and Turkey.

November 28th : the General Assembly adopts a plan for the partition of Palestine which is accepted in principle by the Zionists but rejected by the Arabs.

1948 January 15th : Anglo-Iraqi treaty signed at Portsmouth to replace the treaty of 1930 (not ratified by Baghdad because of mass opposition).

May 15th : Britain relinquishes the mandate and withdraws its forces from Palestine. The Palestine war ensues. The state of Israel is proclaimed at Tel Aviv and is immediately recognized *de facto* by the United States and the Soviet Union.

1949 February 24th–July 20th : the Palestine armistices.

March 30th : Colonel Husni Zaim seizes power in Damascus.

June 15th : Husni Zaim proclaims the 'Cairo-Damascus-Riyad triangle'.

August 4th : the Western Powers condemn the arms race between Arabs and Israelis.

August 14th : Husni Zaim assassinated in fresh military coup.

December 9th : the General Assembly adopts a plan for the internationalization of Jerusalem.

December 19th : a third coup brings Colonel Adib Shishakli to power in Damascus.

1950 April 13th : Arab defence pact framed by the members of the Arab League.

May 25th : Anglo-Franco-American tripartite declaration on the maintenance of the *status quo* in the Middle East (rejected by the Arabs on June 21st).

September 5th : a new Syrian constitution formulates the hope that the Arab nation will become a single united state.

1951 March 15th–20th: the Iranian Parliament votes for nationalization of all oil concessions.

June 18th: Saudi Arabia renews for five years (renewable) American rights to use the air base at Dhahran.

July 20th: assassination of King Abdullah of Jordan in the al-Aksa mosque, in Jerusalem.

October 8th: Nahas Pasha unilaterally denounces the Anglo-Egyptian treaty of 1936. Beginning of guerilla operations against the British forces in the Canal Zone.

October 13th: the Western Powers and Turkey (with American encouragement) invite Egypt to join a Western defence organization (M.E.D.O.) in the Middle East. Egypt at once refuses.

1952 February 18th: the Turkish National Assembly votes in favour of joining the North Atlantic Treaty Organization.

July 26th: 'free officers' eject King Farouk and seize power in Egypt.

November 21st–23rd: attempted popular rising in Baghdad, supported by the army and the police.

1954 February 25th: Colonel Gamal Abdel Nasser supplants General Neguib.

February 27th: General Adib Shishakli relinquishes power. Syria reverts to a parliamentary régime.

April 2nd: Turco-Pakistan agreement of Friendship and Co-operation.

April 21st: Iraqi-American military agreement.

May 10th: Pakistan-American military agreement.

July 27th: Heads of agreement for British evacuation of the Suez Canal Zone initialled in Cairo.

September 19th–20th: rights to exploit oil in southern Iran, formerly held by the Anglo-Iranian Oil Company, granted to an international consortium.

September 29th–October 4th: first successes of the left, and in particular of the Baath party, in the Syrian Parliamentary elections.

October 19th: signature of Anglo-Egyptian agreement for the withdrawal of British troops from the Canal Zone with a right of re-occupation in the event of war, and agreement to consult in the event of a threat of war, against an Arab state or Turkey.

October 26th: Colonel Nasser unhurt in an attempt on his

life by a member of the Moslem Brotherhood at Alexandria.

1955 February 24th: Turco-Iraqi pact of mutual co-operation signed at Baghdad (the Baghdad Pact).

April 5th: Britain accedes to the Baghdad Pact and as part of the operation reaches a special defence agreement with Iraq to take the place of the treaty of 1930.

September 23rd: Pakistan adheres to the Baghdad Pact.

September 27th: President Nasser announces the supply of arms to the Arabs by the Soviet block, without strings.

October 20th: Syria-Egyptian mutual defence pact.

October 25th: Iran adheres to the Baghdad Pact.

October 27th: Saudi-Egyptian mutual defence pact.

1956 January 16th: authoritarian constitution promulgated in Egypt.

March 1st: dismissal of Glubb Pasha by King Hussein of Jordan.

April 21st: military agreement between Egypt, Saudi Arabia and Yemen.

July 19th: John Foster Dulles notifies the Egyptian ambassador of the withdrawal of American offers to finance the high dam at Aswan.

July 26th: Nasser announces the nationalization of the Suez canal.

October 21st: election of a pro-Egyptian Parliament in Jordan.

October 23rd: formation of a working military coalition by Egypt, Syria and Jordan.

October 29th: Israel starts preventive military action in Sinai.

October 30th: London and Paris urge a cease-fire on Israel and Egypt.

October 31st: British and French bombardment of Egyptian airfields.

November 6th: having taken Port Said, Anglo-French forces cease operations at the behest of the United Nations, who decide to despatch an international force.

December 31st: the President of the U.S.A. enunciates the broad outline of the Eisenhower Doctrine for the development of the Middle East.

1957 February 11th: the U.S.S.R. proposes to the West a quadripartite declaration on the Middle East.

March 9th : confirmation and publication of the Eisenhower Doctrine.

March 12th–May 7th : the Richards mission to the Middle East to collect accessions to the Eisenhower Doctrine.

March 16th : American-Lebanese communiqué endorsing the Eisenhower Doctrine.

March 23rd : U.S.A. joins military committee of the Baghdad Pact. U.S. Sixth Fleet in eastern Mediterranean.

March–April : riots in Jordan against the Baghdad Pact.

April 10th : King Hussein of Jordan dismisses the pro-Egyptian Nabulsi cabinet and (15th) installs a moderate government.

May 4th–5th : fresh socialist successes in Syrian bye-elections.

July 5th : Syrian Parliament expresses its wish for union with Egypt.

August 6th : important agreement for technical and economic aid to Syria obtained in Moscow by Khaled al-Azm.

September 3rd : Syrian-Egyptian agreement on economic union.

October 13th : Egyptian troops land at Latakia to support Syria which feels itself threatened by Turkey.

October 21st : Damascus refuses Saudi Arabian mediation.

December 28th : opening of Afro-Asian conference in Cairo.

1958 January 29th : extensive Russo-Egyptian agreement on technical co-operation.

February 1st : Egypt and Syria create the United Arab Republic.

February 14th : federation of the Hashemite Kingdoms of Iraq and Jordan as the 'Arab Union'.

March 8th : federation of Yemen and the United Arab Republic.

March 21st : delegation of powers by King Saud to emir Feisal.

May 7th : assassination at Beirut of an opposition journalist, Nassib Metni. Onset of crisis in the Lebanon.

May 13th : Russo-Egyptian communiqué at the conclusion of President Nasser's visit to the U.S.S.R. confirms a wide range of agreement.

July 14th : proclamation of a republic in Baghdad following a military coup. Assassination of Feisal II and Nuri ai-Said.

July 16th: American forces land in Lebanon and British parachutists occupy Amman airfield. (Withdrawn October 26th–30th.)

II. SOME OIL STATISTICS

1. Oil Production (in millions of tons)

	1914	1930	1938	1947	1954	1956	1957	1958	1959
Kuwait	—	—	—	2·2	47·72	54·98	57·30	70·21	70·00
Saudi Arabia	—	—	—	12·1	46·87	47·87	49·00	50·10	53·60
Iraq	—	0·1	4·8	4·5	30·66	31·32	21·00	35·69	41·70
Iran	0·4	5·8	10·5	20·4	3·00	26·53	35·50	40·59	45·50
Qatar	—	—	—	—	4·78	5·88	6·50	8·22	8·15
Egypt	0·1	0·3	0·2	1·3	1·99	1·80	2·00	2·55	3·60
Bahrein	—	—	0·6	1·5	1·50	1·50	1·67	2·04	2·25
Kuwait neutral zone	—	—	—	—	0·85	1·60	3·48	4·26	6·00
Turkey	—	—	—	—	0·05	0·30	0·30	0·30	0·33
Israel	—	—	—	—	—	0·03	0·07	0·09	0·13
Middle East total	0·5	6·2	16·2	42·0	137·42	171·81	176·82	214·05	231·26

2. Oil Transit

A. By pipeline to the Mediterranean

<table>
<tr><th>From</th><th>To</th><th>Companies concerned</th><th>Date of opening</th><th>Normal annual capacity (million tons)</th></tr>
<tr><td>Kirkuk, Iraq</td><td>Haifa, Israel</td><td>I.P.C.</td><td>1931</td><td>—</td></tr>
<tr><td>Kirkuk, Iraq</td><td>Tripoli, Lebanon</td><td>I.P.C.</td><td>1931</td><td rowspan="2">7·5</td></tr>
<tr><td>Kirkuk, Iraq</td><td>Tripoli, Lebanon</td><td>I.P.C.</td><td>1950</td></tr>
<tr><td>Hassa, Saudi Arabia</td><td>Saida, Lebanon</td><td>Tapline</td><td>1950</td><td>15·5</td></tr>
<tr><td>Kirkuk, Iraq</td><td>Banias, Syria</td><td>I.P.C.</td><td>195[illegible]</td><td>10·5</td></tr>
</table>

B. By the Suez Canal

Westbound crude oil in 1955 (the last normal year before the Suez crisis) was 66·89 million tons out of a total south–north traffic of 87·43 million tons and a world total of 107·51 million tons.

3. Major International Producers

Country	Companies concerned	Interests represented (in percentages)	
Kuwait	Kuwait Oil	G.O. (A)	50
		B.P. (B)	50
Saudi Arabia	Aramco	S.O.C. (A)	30
		S.O.N.J. (A)	30
		T.O. (A)	30
		S.M. (A)	10
Iraq	Iraq Petroleum and associated companies	B.P. (B)	23·75
		R.D.S. (D)	23·75
		C.F.P. (F)	23·75
		S.O.N.J. (A)	11·87
		S.M. (A)	11·87
		G.E. (P)	5·00
Iran	Iranian Oil Exploration and Producing Company	B.P. (B)	40
		R.D.S. (D)	14
		S.O.C. (A)	7
		S.O.N.J. (A)	7
		T.O. (A)	7
		S.M. (A)	7
		G.O. (A)	7
		C.F.P. (F)	6
		I. (A)	5
Qatar	Iraq Petroleum through Petroleum Development (Qatar)	See above	
Egypt	Anglo-Egyptian Oilfields	B.P. (B)	30
		R.D.S. (D)	30
		Egyptian government	10
		(P)	30
	Mobiloil Egypt	M.O. (A)	100
Bahrein	Bahrein Petroleum	S.O.C. (A)	50
		T.O. (A)	50
Neutral zone	American Independent Oil Pacific Western Oil	I. (A)	100

This table includes only countries where production exceeded one million tons in 1957. (See Key on page 213)

KEY

(A)	American	(F)	French
(B)	British	(P)	Various private
(D)	Dutch		

B.P.	British Petroleum	M.O.	Mobiloil Overseas Oil
C.F.P.	Compagnie française des pétroles	R.D.S.	Royal Dutch Shell
G.E.	Gulbenkian Estates	S.M.	Socony Mobiloil
G.O.	Gulf Oil	S.O.C.	Standard Oil of California
I.	Independent American producers	S.O.N.J.	Standard Oil of New Jersey
		T.O.	Texas Oil

INDEX

Index

N

O

P

Q

R

S